China Travel Guide

Contemporary Notes From China by Tara Goldsmith

(A Travel Guide to Make the Most Out of Your Journey in China)

Casey Weaver

Published By **Jackson Denver**

Casey Weaver

China Travel Guide: Contemporary Notes From China by Tara Goldsmith (A Travel Guide to Make the Most Out of Your Journey in China)

ISBN 978-1-998769-55-1

No part of this guidebook shall be reproduced in any form without permission in writing from the publisher except in the case of brief quotations embodied in critical articles or reviews.

Legal & Disclaimer

The information contained in this ebook is not designed to replace or take the place of any form of medicine or professional medical advice. The information in this ebook has been provided for educational & entertainment purposes only.

The information contained in this book has been compiled from sources deemed reliable, and it is accurate to the best of the Author's knowledge; however, the Author cannot guarantee its accuracy and validity and cannot be held liable for any errors or omissions. Changes are periodically made to this book. You must consult your doctor or get professional medical advice before using any of the suggested remedies, techniques, or information in this book.

Upon using the information contained in this book, you agree to hold harmless the Author from and against any damages, costs, and expenses, including any legal fees potentially resulting from the application of any of the information provided by this guide. This disclaimer applies to any damages or injury caused by the use and application, whether directly or indirectly, of any advice or information presented, whether for breach of contract, tort, negligence, personal injury, criminal intent, or under any other cause of action.

You agree to accept all risks of using the information presented inside this book. You need to consult a professional medical practitioner in order to ensure you are both able and healthy enough to participate in this program.

Table Of Contents

Chapter 1: Architectural History

Chinese history, culture and religion have always been closely connected to architecture. Architecture has changed over time due to the religious beliefs and practices of its inhabitants, which were often influenced heavily by their ruling dynasties.

As early as 7,000 years old, the Chinese invented many simple building techniques. Their houses ranged from cave dwellings, which can still be inhabited today, to holes dug in the ground with thatch roofs. Around 2100 BC, packed earth houses appeared. These homes were raised from the ground with mounds and compact mud.

China was able to see more sophisticated architecture at work with the Zhou Dynasty. New styles of building such as feng-shui were popularized. To support their tyrannical ways of rule, the Qin Dynasty built even more stunning buildings. Buddhism brought with it new styles of architecture.

With the advent of the Tang and Song, architecture got more complex and intricate with elaborate sculptures, multieaved roofs and finer interior decoration. The Chinese style was the most popular, with the exception of the Ming and Qing. They were the ones who built huge structures such as The Forbidden Town, the Temple of Heaven, the Royal Summer Palace, and many others.

Chinese architecture has been inspired and influenced by Buddhist, Imperial and Islamic architecture. The sheer complexity of the architecture throughout history is enough for anyone to go googly eyed. China is beautiful and has lots to offer architects who love architectural beauty.

Chapter 2: Understanding Chinese History and Religion

Chronology of Chinese Dynasties

Chinese history is filled with emperors. Chinese history has 6,000 years worth of history. Each period serves to be a role model and twists like a dragon.

A dynasty can be defined as a period during which a ruling body held the territory. Its roots date back to the Neolithic Period. This was when the people lived within communities ruled and governed by chieftains. These chieftains were seen as a source of help for religious, political, or social needs. A new leader takes the place of the previous leader. Usually, it was brother to sister or nephew or uncle until the male family members became exhausted or were overthrown.

These family lines could survive for decades or even generations. As territories grew, so did their power. The role of the leaders changed from that of chieftains to kings to eventually emperors. A dynasty would refer to the length of time that a family ruled.

These dynasties can be established by proving the legitimacy of their rulers through the Mandate of Heaven. The Mandate allowed gods to rule. Yu, the first emperor of Xia Dynasty was said to be given the Mandate of Heaven when he overthrew the corrupt last of five mythical emperors. His descendants were able to continue to rule but their corrupt behavior led to the Mandate of Heaven being taken from them and given to the Shang.

For many people who wanted to achieve power, it was complicated to find out if the Mandate had been removed. Natural disasters like floods, famines and earthquakes along with peasant revolts would reduce the social and political prestige of an Emperor, making them vulnerable to attack. The most vulnerable people to them, such as generals, would often take control and establish a new kingdom. Natural disasters were used to prove that they have the divine right. This strategy proved extremely effective and was used right up to the end of imperial China.

The general public believes that there are only 17 Dynasties in which the entirety of Chinese history can fit into. It is not true. These dynasties often overlapped, and there were probably more than 100 self declared dynasties than 17, with some being established by non Han Chinese rulers. Historical experts consider only 17 to be 'legitimate.

With each dynasty, their time ruled and the territories they held changed. Some dynasties were short-lived, others lasted decades. In China, today, dynasties could rule half, or even less of the country. Some dynasties like the Song shared their country and territories with non-Han kingdoms.

But no matter how long they ruled or how large the land they controlled, each successive Dynasty served as an example for the next. Emperors would look up the previous rulers as an example of how to live up to them or avoid the mistakes that led them to their demise.

Xia (2200 – 1700 BCE).

While the Xia dynasty is often considered a mythical time that Chinese used to explain their origins for a long period of time, archaeological finds at Banpo (near Xi'an) and other sites have shown evidence that they may have existed. Banpo has shown evidence of a Neolithic agricultural community, which could have been the driving force behind Bronze Age Shang.

Shang (1700 - 1100 BCE):

In 1899, a peasant working near Anyang discovered turtle shells with characters scratched onto them. Archaeologists were called to discover the archaeological existence the Shang dynasty. The Shang culture flourished all over the country's northern regions, including Shandong to Shaanxi and Hebei to Henan. The rulers were semi-divine kings who were supported by various officials and peasants. These were used to create magnificent monuments. Their artisans were extremely skilled and created some of the most famous bronze bells.

Zhou (11100 - 221 BCE).

The Zhou Dynasty is divided into the Western Zhou (11100 - 771 BCE), and the Eastern Zhou (970 - 221 BCE). Their dynasty was established after the first Zhou ruler, a Shaanxi provincial native, killed and succeeded the previous Shang ruler. Their territory grew to include Beijing and the Yangtze, in the south. The Zhou established the feudal structure to help control this large territory. The Zhou period was quickly thrown into chaos. China was divided up into various states during the Eastern Zhou

Dynasty. They also saw continuous battles known collectively as the Warring States. Despite all these turbulent times and wars it was a time in which philosophy and religion thrived. It was also when Confucius, the great scholar, came to dominate every aspect Chinese culture.

Qin (221 BCE-207 BCE)

China's first dynasty of imperial power was formed under Qin Shi Huangdi. This brought an end to the Warring States period. He not only won the nation by sword, but he also ruled according to it. He was the first to introduce legalism. It was a philosophy that emphasized law and punishment. Following his death, however, the country fell into chaos. His youngest son, Liu Bang (a common name) took the throne. However, he committed suicide after being advised by Liu Bang.

Han (206 BCE to 220 CE).

The longest Chinese history, the Han Dynasty, expanded China's territory and power through the incorporation of outsider kingdoms into its empire. The introduction of an examination system and Confucian education were promoted. This dynasty's most notable feature was the establishment the Silk Road. It led to new inventions in technology and religions.

Three Kingdoms (220 to 80 BCE).

The Era of Disunity, also known as the Three Kingdoms, began when the Han family fell into social and political decline. People fled to the south to escape from the bloodshed, which was short, brutal, and difficult. Three kingdoms existed: Wei (220 to 65), Shu (221 to 633) and Wu (229 to 80).

Jin (265 CE – 420 CE)

Separated into the Western Jin (265-317) and the Eastern Jin (317-420), the Jindynasty, which was established by the Jurchen (ancestors of Manchus in north

China), was established. While the political scene was peaceful for a while, it did not last long. China fell back into competition for power and the Jin became the next dynasty.

Southern and Northern Dynasties (420-589 CE)

The Southern and Northern Dynasties were a time in which bloodshed was intensified and people's lifespans were cut. The Song (420-79) and Qi (479-502), Qi (552-52) and Liang (502-572) comprised the Southern Dynasties. Chen (557-89) was also included. The Northern Dynasties comprised the Northern Wei (386-534), Eastern Wei (550-50), Northern Qi 550-77, Western Wei (535-56) & the Northern Zhou (5557-81).

Sui (581 - 618 CE):

The country was united once more under a Han Chinese administration during this period. While it would only last a few years, it would experience many great accomplishments. One of these was the Grand Canal. The collapse of the Korean military campaigns and the other countries in the country would result in the demise of the dynasty. They also created very strong enemies.

Tang (618 - 907):

The Tang Dynasty is the shining star of Chinese history. It quickly and easily gained new territory and made enemies tremble. Many rulers from Asia would pay tribute, including one female emperor in Chinese historical history.

Five Dynasties and Ten Kingdoms (907 - 60 CE).

China was quickly in chaos. Once again, the country was soon divided up and ruled over by different kings. Later Liang (907–23), Later Tang (923–36), Later Jin (946–47), Later Han (947-50), Later Zhou (51)

Liao (907 - 1125 CE):

The Liao period was established by the Liao dynasty by the northern Khitans. These Khitans were considered barbarians by the Han Chinese. The Liao period ruled roughly within the same timeline as the Chinese Song, according to later Chinese records.

Song Dynasty (960 - 1279 CE):

China was finally reunited again after a long period. But the territory was much smaller than it was prior to that. It would then be broken into two periods, the Northern Song (960-1127) as well as the Southern Song (1127-1279). Genghis Khan's Mongolian army and Genghis Khan would witness major technological, economic, and political developments in Song dynasty.

Jin Dynasty (1115 – 1234 CE).

Not to be confused by the earlier Jin period. This Jin Dynasty was founded, flourished and then fell while the Song were still in power. Also known as The Jurchen Dynasty or the Northern Semi-nomadic Tribe, it was founded to overthrow Liao Dynasty. It fell to the power of the Mongolian Army soon after.

Yuan Dynasty (1279 - 1368 CE):

Kublai Khan, the great-grandson of Genghis Khan founded officially the Yuan Dynasty. Genghis Kan had control over parts of China, so the actual dates should be 1206 -1368. The rulers were Mongolian but they supported Chinese art and used Chinese government to rule. However, their power quickly diminished due to natural catastrophes such as revolts and plagues. Soon they were pushed back to Mongolia.

Ming (1368-1644CE):

The Ming period, which was the last Han Chinese monarchy to rule, is famous for the lengthening and fortifying of the Great Wall. This was the period that saw the creation of Neo-Confucianism, promotion of fine arts, and the increase in wealth. However, political turmoil and natural hazards soon weakened the Ming rulers. The northern Manchus then saw the opportunity to invade.

Qing (1644 – 1911 CE)

The Manchus are the last imperial Chinese dynasty. They were the descendants the Jurchen, who established two dynasties during previous centuries. They were resentful of the Han Chinese who forced them to adopt the Manchu hairstyle. It consisted of a shaved face and a long braid known as a queue. The country was encouraged to continue the arts and gained more territorial power. However foreign incursions and rebellions as well natural disasters led to their fall.

Chinese dynasties are widely recognized as the oldest civilization still standing. This allows for a wonderful insight into a well-loved culture, and the rise of a powerful country. Each dynasty would receive recognition for its achievements and mistakes, as well as being a strong reminder for future historians.

The establishment and maintenance of the Han Dynasty, China

The fall and establishment of Han dynasty are the underlying causes. Qin Shi Huangdi, also known as the First Chinese Emperor, ruled over the country with an iron fist. Drinking beverages to make him immortal led to his congestive heart disease and death in c.210 CE.

Zhao Gao, the Han Dynasty founder, was buried in the name of his father. In these documents, it was stated his younger son, Prince Huhai to assume the reins and Fusi, his older son (who in fact was the legitimate heir), was charged with treason. Fusi was ordered to commit suicide.

Within six months, chaos erupted in the country and rebellions were spread across the nation. The people claimed they had the right and authority to overthrow an imperial house which had clearly lost Heaven's Mandate. Zhao Gao had taken Qin Eri Shi (Second Imperial) the young prince and manipulated it.

Zhao Gao was finally done with the hiding place of the Second Emperor in 207 BCE. Zhao Gao saw the Second Emperor hiding away and declared that an army was waiting to kill him. Qin Eri Shi did not know what to say and Zhao Gao suggested that Zhao Gao kill himself. Zhao Gao was killed quickly after the Second Emperor consumed the poison, which he had been given by his trusted advisor. Thus ended the Qin Dynasty.

The following four years were marked by political unrest, bloody battles and political turmoil. China had a power vacuum and many were trying to fill it. Chen She, a Chu-based ploughman was the first challenger. The order to go to the frontier was given to him in 209 BCE. But heavy rain made it impossible to reach his destination so he turned around and stated that deserters would be treated harshly. His call for Great Chu to rise again was heard, and others were soon persuaded by him to come along. The cry of 'Great Chu shall rise again' quickly changed into 'Chen She's king'.

His conscripts were quickly converted into an army. It was highly Anti-Qin. He founded the ancient state Chu, and declared himself king. Sima Qian would name him the Melancholy Queen. But he was attacked and killed by his own men in less than a year.

Another man would step forward, another peasant called Liu Bang. He was modeled after Chen She. Liu Bang came from the same state as the king, Chu, and was subject to brigandage. However, he gained an auspicious reputation quickly.

After Chen She's demise, it became Xiang Yu, who declared himself king. He was a strong commander, and aligned his self with

Liu Bang. Xiang Yu, a powerful commander, inflicted a series of heavy and decisive defeats on Qin strongholds the year after the Second Emperor committed suicide.

Liu Bang also led his men westward and northward to Qin. He was able to make contact with the Qin Court because the passes were more easily defended. He quickly learned of the death the Second Emperor. The 'Third Imperial', the grandson Qin Shi Huangdi as well as the son of Prince Fusi, encouraged him. Liu Bang marched forward to take the capital, despite not consulting Xiang Yu.

Xiang Yu got furious and marched toward Xiangyang. He encamps his 40,000 soldiers within a day of Liu Bang's 100,000. In addition to his anger at Liu Bang's insubordination, there were rumors Xiang Yu had made a deal, which was further emphasized by the fact, that he had treated both the people and the Emperor very well.

Liu Bang reported personally to his commander after reconciliation was initiated. Although the loyalties of both were confirmed, Liu Bang was able to excuse himself and sneak out from camp to return to his own army. Xiang Yu was a furious emperor and his anger had no limits. The First Emperor was killed, and the First Emperor's tomb was looted. Xiang Yu's army then supplied his warriors with the Terracotta Warriors to help them fight.

Xiang Yu decided to return home rather than establishing power at Qin stronghold. The Qin State was divided into four regions. Liu Bang received Ba and Shu (modern-day Sichuan Province) in the belief it would keep him busy and away from trouble. He was then proclaimed King of Han in the year 206 BCE. This began the Han kingdom. His dynasty would last four years.

Liu Bang did not see this area as a place for exile. He saw it as a sanctuary. To ensure that he would not be followed, Liu Bang dismantled Stone Cattle Road as well many other mountainous roads.

Liu Bang had already closed the roads but they were again opened to let in 560,000 men. He won the battle and took Pengcheng as Chu capital. Xiang Yu learned of the news and quickly rushed to help. With only 30,000 men he retook the capital.

Liu Bang ought to have been captured. But a duststorm saved him from being captured and allowed him to escape. His family was captured. Once more he was surrounded and only able to flee twice. Xiang Yu threatened Liu Bang to kill his father in 203 BCE. However, Liu Bang was not apathetic. Later in the year, the two sides traded insults, and his father was freed.

Gaixia was in modern Anhui and the battle to decide everything was fought there. Xiang Yu's army had drained most of its resources and was surrounded Liu Bang's men. According to reports, many of Xiang

Yu's troops defected and joined Liu Bang. With the help of his beautiful wife Yu and 800 men, he got on to his horse and rode south to escape.

He had reduced his 800 men to 28 when they reached Yangtze River. However, he promised them victory. A promise he kept. They were waiting for a boat to ferry them to safety. But he felt embarrassed and dismounted, and he returned to the Han soldiers. He fought bravely and killed many. However, when he recognized a captain of the cavalry, he cut his own throat.

Liu Bang became the Supreme Emperor of China, and not the King or Han, on the 28th February, 202 BCE. This is when he adopted his posthumous imperial title Gaozu. His rise to prominence from a simple peasant and founding a kingdom from obscurity would continue to influence subsequent peasants.

Introduction to Ancient Chinese Religion

Over the years, many religions have influenced the Chinese people. These diverse faiths have influenced their lives. They provide an explanation of what has happened, how they live their lives, and what will happen after death.

The three main religions that have dominated Chinese history are Confucianism Buddhism, Daoism and Buddhism. Where the founders of all three have been defied, they have become the foundations of many other religions. The Chinese religious landscape has also been enriched by a variety of other religions such as animalism, ancestral worship and shamanism.

Confucianism

Confucianism (Rujia sixiang), is more of a philosophy that a religion. However, it has over time become intertwined to pre-existing faiths, making it one China's most influential faiths.

Confucianism developed from the beliefs held by Confucius (Master Kong/Kong Fuzi). Born in 551 BCE during the Warring states era of the Zhou Dynasty. Born to a poor household in the State of Lu (modern-day Shandong Province), he had hoped to hold a high ranking position in government. Unfortunately, he only managed to secure a few minor posts.

At 50, he was obsessed with his God-given purpose in life: to persuade leaders of the various states to live a life of virtue. He spent 13 year traveling from one state in another, offering unrestricted advice to rulers. His hope was that someone would take his advice. They didn't succeed and he returned home to spend five years teaching and editing classic literature. He then died in 479 BCE. Mencius (372-289 BCE), who was his son, published Confucius' beliefs and ideas in The Book of Mencius. The philosophy would have a profound impact on China and many other Asian countries.

Confucianism's central theme revolves around how human relationships can lead to harmony and virtue. The foundation of a harmonious community was built on the five relationships promoted by Confucianism: husband and wives, husband and wife and father and son, ruler, subject, elder, younger and friends. Confucian texts would have an influence on the country's administration. They were meant to be a set of morals to guide everyone, even the emperor.

Daoism

Daoism (Daojiao), the Chinese religion which originated in China, is Daoism. According to tradition, the founder of Daoism was Laotzu (Laotze Laotze Laozi), a man born sometime in 607 BC. Some believe he died in his lifetime because a lot of his life isn't known, even his real identity.

Laotzu had been told that he rode his water buffalo to Tibet in order to contemplate in solitude as he approached the end. The gatekeeper requested that he leave behind a record of what he believed. The book, which was only 5000 words, became one of the most famous books in the Far East. It is called the Tao Te Ching (The Book of the Way).

Daoism's central theme, Tao, is Dao. Dao (or Tao; both are accepted) can only been recognized through spiritual self awareness. Because it transcends the senses, imagination, and will not be lost, It can't be expressed simply with words. Laotzu's book begins with the statement that any Dao can be expressed only in words. Dao is nature's way, it is what drives the universe and gives life meaning and purpose.

Daoism eventually split into two parts - philosophical Daoism or religious Daoism. Confucianism was incorporated into religious Daoism. The focus of this branch is on immortality and what happens after death. Daoist priests were successful in exorcising demons and evil spirits. This allowed them to build a large number of gods, goddesses or spirits. Philosophical Daoism on the other side became a way for sages to escape the world of man and live in solitude.

Buddhism

Siddhartha Guitama (563 - 483 BCE) founded Buddhism in India. He was a prince who had lived a comfortable and luxurious life. His teachings became popular in China during the 1st century CE.

Buddhism centers on the belief that all human life is subject to suffering, from conception to death. This is why desire is at the root of evil. Desire is disillusionment, and happiness can only be achieved by getting rid of this illusion. To achieve this, you must follow the eightfold route, the path to Nirvana.

Buddhism was initially not popular among Chinese people. It was because they were used to worshipping idols and gods while Buddhism didn't really have any. Buddhism taught that filial penitence was not allowed. Another reason was the fact that Buddhism, which was fundamentally a foreign religion was considered a threat for the Chinese identity, which was firmly grounded within Confucianism. After a while, Buddhism was able to build a loyal following. However, several emperors prohibited it throughout the various dynasties.

Over the centuries Buddhism split into several branches, including Indian, Chinese Zen Zen, Theravada Mahayana and Zen. All of them had a significant impact on lives, as well as on the religious and political landscape. It is now the most prominent religion in China.

Islam

The Prophet Mohammed (Yislan Jiao), the founder of Islam was born around 560 CE. His name translates to highly praised. When he was alive, there were many gods and goddesses in the Middle East. His declaration that Allah was the only god created a sensation. His vision of brotherhood was met with violent reactions by others.

He was forced to leave Medina in 622 and was exiled there. But he established a solid political foundation, and a military. He conquered Mecca then brought the rest Arabia to his control, before he died in 632.

Islam gained a very strong foothold in China quite peacefully. Arab traders ventured into Asia via the maritime connections to Guangzhou and Quanzhou. They also used the Silk Road. They converted a large portion of Han Chinese as well the Uighur's, a Chinese group with Turkish ancestry. This makes up approximately 5% today of the religious population.

Ancestral Worship

The ancient form of worship that China has used is ancestral worship. Centuries ago, worshipping one's ancestors in religious rituals was a common practice in China. It was initially only the elite who offered sacrifices or prayers to their ancestors, but as time went by, more people began to do this. Today, it is common to pay tributes to your ancestors among all classes.

Religion played an important role for the Chinese people. It provided them with a way to understand the world and explain why things happen. Each religion and philosophy has taken elements form other faiths and integrated them into their own canon. Chinese religions are diverse and fascinating, just like the people.

Chapter 3: Tourist Hotspots

Great Wall of China

Of course, I was going mention the Great Wall of China! You'd have seen it coming. It is impossible to talk about China without mentioning this magnificent structure.

The Great Wall of China has been named one of the Seven Wonders of the World. It extends over 21,000 kilometers from east to west in China. There are many difficult terrains it will encounter, but the Great Wall is able to traverse grasslands and deserts as well as mountains. Although parts of the wall have been partially or totally destroyed by nature, they are still some of the most impressive and important structures in the nation and the world. It is a World Heritage Site according to UNESCO.

Construction of the Great Wall began during the Warring States Era and continued for over 2000 years, up to the time of Ming Dynasty. It required a large manpower of soldiers, local people, and even prisoner workers. Much of what we see today was built during Ming Dynasty's rule. It was originally intended to be a fortification against the states of Zhao, Yan, Qin. But, it was extended and fixed up throughout the dynasties. Later dynasties saw the consolidation of what was once separate walls. This is when it was renamed "Great Wall".

The Great Wall, which is both impressive and mysterious in its own right, holds great importance in Chinese mythology as well as culture. It is a central part of many folk stories and legends. It is widely considered the greatest feat human engineering. It is also a symbol representing the great wisdom of the people of China.

The Great Wall is over 13,000 miles long and it's impossible for the average tourist to see all of it. I'll list the top parts of the Wall which are most popular with different tourists so that they can really enjoy the beauty of it.

Badaling:

Badaling, which is in Beijing, is the most popular and stunning section of this wall. It is well maintained, and tourists love to view it. It is also the most renovated and safest section. If you are not a fan of crowds or prefer peace and quiet, this section may be best avoided. This section is available as part of many tourist packages to Beijing.

Jinshanling:

This section is quite the opposite to the Badaling. It is unrestored and steeper. It's not popular and there are very few souvenir sellers. It's a great area for photography and adventure.

Mutianyu und Simatai

These sections offer a mixture of sightseeing, adventure, and renovation. They aren't as well developed as Badaling, but they are still safe enough to attract visitors. The Mutianyu section, which is located in Huairou County has lush green forests. It offers breathtaking views in the summer. Simatai can be described as a mix of renovated and ruins, and makes for stunning sights. The eastern section is difficult and should not be climbed by people in poor physical condition.

It is best to visit the Great Wall from May to October for ordinary visitors. It's a pleasant temperature and quite sunny. The best months to visit are May and September when there aren't too many tourists. The temperatures are extremely cold between November and April.

Tibet

Many travelers are drawn to Tibet because of its spiritual and adventurous appeal. Nearly twice the area of France, this region is home to approximately 2.8million people.

Travelers from all around the globe continue to be fascinated by it.

While modern Tibet is still a very poor area in China, it is extremely friendly. The Yarlung Tsangpo is the central part of the province. Here you can find many of the oldest monasteries as well as temples. Lhasa is known for being the place where many Buddhists make pilgrimage to, and for having the former Dalai Lamas. Mount Kailash can also be reached by pilgrimage. This usually takes around one week. This is the holiest area in Tibet so it should not be difficult to reach.

Potala Palace

Potala Palace sits on the Red Hill, central Lhasa. It is an exquisite ancient palace-cum–museum. It's at 3,700 m elevation and is the world's highest ancient palace. It was home to the Dalai Lama up until 1959. It now houses a history museum. It is the core of

Tibetan culture, religion, and politics. It houses many local crafts and gold wares.

Songtsan Gampo, in the 7th century, built the original palace. It had nine floors and a thousand rooms. Potala, after Mount Potalaka (the legendary abode for Buddha of Mercy), was the name of the building. After his dynasty's fall, the palace was abandoned to natural forces and wars which greatly damaged it. It was restored in 17th-century by the Qing Dynasty and is a UNESCO World Heritage property since 1994.

The Potala Palace comprises mainly two main parts. The Red Palace, located in the center of the palace, and the White Palace which forms the wings.

The White Palace, Portrang Karpo

It is the latest part of Palace. It was constructed first by Qing Dynasty, 17th Century during the time the 5th Dalai Lama lived there, and later expanded to its current form by the 13th Dalai Lama at the end of the 20th century. It had living quarters and offices. It also served as the office building of the local government. It has seven floors which were all historically used for various official purposes. It is home to the eight Dalai Lama tombs (also called the golden stupas), as well as numerous shrines, libraries, and scriptures.

The Red Palace, Portrang Marpo

This part of the palace is the highest and is entirely dedicated for religious study. It houses a complex collection of chapels.

The Great West Hall houses four splendid chapels and is the main hall of the Red Palace. It is decorated with fine murals that depict scenes from life of the 5th Dalai Lama. The Saint's Chapel is north of this hall. It is an original 7th century building. There are also four other chapels. They include the North Chapel; the East Chapel; the West Chapel; and the South Chapel. These chapels contain the golden funerary stupas, all of which are studded in gold and gems. They also have various scriptures or sculptures.

You can also visit the main galleries which feature various murals as well as bronze statues and dark areas. There is also a souvenir shop and refreshment pavilion.

Travel Tips Register at least one day in advance to secure your tickets. These tickets are valid for one week. The visiting time is one hour and there is a strict route. It is forbidden to bring oxygen bags or liquids with you. Additionally, only one restroom is available on the entire route. You should bring a warm coat as it can get cold at high altitudes.

Beijing

Ah, Beijing. This is China's capital and it is a place unlike any other. Modern skyscrapers stand side-by-side with ancient monuments. Shopping centers are situated opposite temples dating back from the Yuan Ming and Qing Dynasties. Beijing is a mixture between old and new. With great attractions and historical sites, restaurants and hotels to suit all budgets, it's a perfect destination for singles or couples as well for whole families.

Beijing is filled with historical monuments, historical sites. Beijing's most notable attractions include the Forbidden Garden, Temple of Heaven, Tiananmen Plaza, and many more. There are many museums, art galleries and temples throughout the city that are not often overlooked by the main attractions. However, they are worth a visit. Although Beijing is much bigger than London, Beijing holds many wonderful parks that can help you forget all the noise and hustle of the city and allow for you to relax and enjoy peace and quiet.

Temple of Heaven

The Temple of Heaven also goes by the name Altar of Heaven. It is found in Beijing's southern Dongcheng District. The park was originally built as a palace to host the Heaven Worship Ceremony for the Qing Dynasty rulers. It is now a public park. It was constructed by Emperor Yongle from 1406 to 1402, and then enlarged by Emperor Jiajing (and Emperor Qianlong), who gave it its name, Temple of Heaven. He also built Temple of Moon, Temple of Sun, Temple of Earth, and Temple of the Moon.

The park covers more than 3,529,000 acres, making it China's largest and most representative old sacrificial construction. It is a magnificent example of architecture from the ancient East. It houses over 60,000 tree varieties, the most popular being the 500-year-old Nine Dragon Cypress. The palace became a park when it was transformed into a museum in 1988. It now displays the ancient philosophy, religion and culture of China. A festival of sorts is held in the Temple of Heaven every Lunar, to celebrate Chinese culture. It is full with beautiful music, dance and ceremonies.

Chinese believed the Heaven was higher than the Earth and had a round shape. This is clearly evident in the Temple of Heaven design. The Temple of Heaven is circular, but is higher on one side. The Earth's southern side is more square and lower. There are four gates to the park that can be accessed via public transportation.

Altar of Prayer For Good Harvests

The magnificent building is built on three levels with a marble-stone base. It stands at 38 meters tall and is entirely constructed of wood without the use of nails. It was used by the Emperors to pray for good harvests, pleasant weather, and good luck.

Imperial Vault for Heaven:

The Imperial Vault can be found along the middle axis from South Gate towards North

Heaven Gate. It is smaller than the Hall of Prayer for Good Harvests. It is known for its Echo Wall which surrounds it. This wall can transmit sounds over long distances and makes use of sound wave theories. You will also find the Three Echo Stones as well as the Dialogue Stone.

Palace of Abstinence

This place was especially important for the sacrificial practices. The Heaven Worship Ceremony was started here by the Emperors who fasted. It is located southwest of Altar of Prayer for Good Harvests.

Divine Music Administration

It is located southwest of Palace of Abstinence. It was used as a headquarters for the management body for ceremonial instruments and for planning and rehearsals of the sacrificial ceremonies.

Circular Mound Altar:

Located south of The Imperial Vault of Heaven the Circular Mund Altar is actually the Temple of Heaven. It is where the Ming- and Qing Dynasties' Emperors performed their annual sacrificial acts. It's located on a raised platform. Three levels of carved marble dragons decorate it.

The park is open every day from 6am until 10pm. It has good connection with both the subway and bus. To fully enjoy this park's beauty and grandeur, it is recommended that tourists take at least 2 hours.

Forbidden City

The Forbidden Garden, also known under the Forbidden Palace, got its name from Zijin Cheng (an English translation of its Chinese name). The "forbidden" part refers to that no one was permitted to enter the city without permission from the Emperor. It is commonly called Gugong in China.

The Palace Museum can be found in Beijing's Forbidden Town. Built on 180 acres of land in the early 15th-century during the reign Emperor Chengzu, this palace boasts stunning traditional Chinese architecture. It was home to the Qing and Ming dynasties' 24 emperors. The palace also served as the political centre of the Chinese government over the course of 500 years.

It is believed to have been the work of millions of artisans and workers who brought large amounts of timber, stone, or other materials from distant provinces to the construction sites. Many of the structures found in the palace complex were constructed using unusual materials, such as glutinous rice or egg whites. These buildings are unique.

The overall color of the entire complex is yellow. Yellow is the principal color of royal family. Roofs, tiles as well decorations and bricks are all yellow. The only exception is Wenyuange's royal library, which has an orange roof.

The Forbidden Kingdom is smaller in size than the Temple of Heaven. This is because the Emperors were considered the Sons of Heaven. While the Celestial Emperor ruled the Heaven, his Earthly abode; the Temple of Heaven had the need to be bigger than the dwelling of emperors.

There are many wonderful parts of this complex to explore. The Forbidden Town is UNESCO's World Cultural Heritage site. It is a very popular tourist attraction.

Forbidden Cities visitors need to be aware that only the Meridian Gate gate, on the southern side of the complex, allows entry. You can only go south to north on the unidirectional tour of the complex. The Gate of Divine Might at the north is prohibited.

You must see the palace's splendor when you travel to China.

Sha'anxi Province

China's past and current history can be described as Shaanxi Province. It is China's heartland. The Wei River is the birthplace of the remarkable Chinese civilization. It was also the site of various Neolithic cultures that gave rise to later states, which would eventually become the first dynasties.

Shaanxi Province has a rich culture and fertile soil. Many ancient Chinese sages made their home in the Qinling Mountains. Laotzu is the most well-known. Shaanxi has many iconic monuments, attractions, and historical sites due to its rich history.

Xi'an

Terracotta Army

Terracotta Army also known as Terracotta Warriors and Horses and is a vast collection of terracotta-sculptures in Lintong District. It was discovered by local farmers digging for a water source near the royal grave. They also found some pottery that attracted archaeologists.

Terracotta Army was a form of funerary artwork that was buried together with Emperor Qin Shi Huang of Qin Dynasty, the first Chinese emperor. It was created to guard and accompany the emperor throughout his life after death. The Emperor Qin Shi Huang Mausoleum Site Park is made up of the Terracotta Army and Emperor Qin Shi Huang's Mausoleum.

It is a museum that covers over 16,000 square meter. It is divided in three pits and tagged according their discovery order. Over 8,000 soldiers, more than 650 horses and 130 Chariots can be found in these three pits. Other figures, including musicians, officials, and strongmen have also been discovered buried in pits. These figures are laid out as battle formations. Each rank and their purpose may have different features and heights. Different weapons have been discovered on the site. The restorations have attempted to match their original forms as closely as possible.

It is believed the construction of Mausoleum started in 246BC when Qin Shi Huang was thirteen years old. It took 11 year to complete. Some believe that the emperor was buried with many valuable and sacrificial objects to go along in his afterlife. This is similar to what happened in the mummification process of the Pharaohs.

The Terracotta Army has been listed as a World Cultural Heritage by UNESCO in 1987. It is a must-see for all visitors to China.

There's much more to Xi'an, than the Terracotta Warriors. Within the city walls, there are the Bell towers and Drum towers that date back to the 14th century. You won't regret visiting Xi'an.

Hua Shan

Daoism boasts five sacred mountains, Hua Shan one of them. Hua Shan will bring you light and a sense of renewal. North Peak is at the top of the mountain. It is here that sages can become one in the infinite. There are three ways up the mountain. Each route offers stunning temples, shrines, and scenic areas. The reward is spectacular views.

Hangcheng

Hangcheng is a famous place because it was the birthplace of Sima Qian. This man wrote the Records of the Grand Historian. There are so many things to do in this area. You can visit the Confucius Temple or the Danjiacun Village. And, of course, you must see the Tomb Of Sima Qian.

Yan'an

Yan'an is the Chinese communist Promised Land. It also marks the spot where Chairman Mao's famous rule. Yan'an, the ending point of Long March 1935, was also the location where Chairman Mao's infamous rule took place. This place is proud of its communist history. Visit the Yangjialing Revolution Headquarters Site to see the dugouts where Mao Zedong and other leaders lived. Also visit the Wangjiaping Revolution

Headquarters Site. And the Yan'an Revolution Museum. If you're looking for more ancient items to see, you will not be disappointed. Treasure Pagoda Ten Thousand Buddha Cave, Qingling Mountain and Treasure Pagoda are all excellent places to see.

Yulin

Yulin is an ancient fortress and still retains its old charm. Beacon Tower May is a great place to visit. Also, you can wander around the streets and take in the views of the old buildings.

Hong Kong

Hong Kong is an amazing combination of East-West, and it's a breath of fresh oxygen. Before becoming a British colony in 1867, the island was home to small fishing villages. In the end, it became one of the most populous metropolises on the planet.

Skyscrapers sit next to traditional apartment blocks. Traditional Chinese shops can also be found on the same street. Designer boutiques as well as vibrant night markets provide a myriad of cultural experiences. The breathtaking views of the Kowloon island and mainland will make you swoon.

Victoria Harbor

Victoria Harbor, which is a natural landscape harbor, is the biggest in China and the third-largest in the world. It is located between Kowloon Peninsula & Hong Kong Island. This makes Hong Kong one of most busiest cities in the globe. Its strategic position was key to Hong Kong becoming a major trading center and British Colony. The British Queen Victoria named the harbor after her reign.

Victoria Harbor is an internationally famous tourist location. It is especially well-known for its amazing panoramic night view. It is listed among the three best night views anywhere in the world. It is home to many skyscrapers on the Hong Kong Island shore, which makes for a breathtaking night view. Here are several public shows, including an annual fireworks display. It is a popular spot for tourists as well as local residents. The shows are also available on TV.

A Symphony of Lights

A Symphony of Lights is the show that you must see. It has been listed in Guinness Book of World Records, as the biggest permanent light and soundshow in the world. It was established by the local Tourism Board as a way to encourage more tourists to the city. It displays more than 40 skyscrapers nightly in a stunning performance.

Golden Bauhinia Square:

The Golden Bauhinia Square is found on Wan Chai, near the Hong Kong Convention and Exhibition Centre. It offers great views as it is surrounded from three sides by Victoria Harbor.

Victoria Peak

Victoria Harbor, without Victoria Peak is impossible! Mount Austin is also known to be Victoria Peak. It's located in the western portion of Hong Kong Island and rises to a height of more than 560 meters. It offers stunning views of the harbor and the city. The Victoria Tower is built there. Annually, seven million people visit The Peak. There are viewing decks and shopping centres on the Peak that allow you to enjoy breathtaking views.

Sichuan Province

Sichuan, although it's not hot in terms or elements (water would be the volcano), is very hot for its delicious spicy cuisine. Because of the use of hot peppers in many dishes, Sichuan is thought to reduce the dampness inside due to high humidity and the rainy weather.

Sichuan Province makes a great place to spend a couple of days. This is China's oldest region. The discovery and preservation of the Shang Dynasty culture Sanxingdui made it a prominent tourist destination. Sichuan offers so many wonderful places that you'll need to spend at least four days exploring them all.

Chengdu

Chengdu, the capital of Sichuan Province, is home to the Giant Pandas. Sichuan Province, also known as Tian Fu Zhi Guio or the Heavenly State, is home to the Giant Pandas. It is blessed with abundant natural resources which makes it highly productive. Two branches from the Yangtze River are responsible for irrigation of an area measuring 270 square miles. They are the Min River and the Tuo River.

The remarkable thing about Chengdu, is its solid presence in history. It can be traced back as far back as 2,400 year ago. The capital city of Sichuan since thousands of year, Chengdu has not had its name changed. It was the heart of politics and business in the region. Its handicraft industries are well-known for the high quality material they produce.

Chengdu is renowned for its Giant Panda Breeding Research Base. Visitors can also enjoy a wide range of activities and events. Tourists are recommended to visit a teahouse, and then go to an Opera performance. Chunxi Road is a great place to shop if your interest is in shopping. The street food in Chengdu is also worth a try. It is spicy, hot and absolutely delicious.

Chengdu Research Base For Giant Panda Breeding

This research base is also known by the Chengdu Panda Base. It was founded in 1987. It serves the main purpose of breeding giant pandas and other rare species. The research base is designed to provide the best environment for these animals in order that they can breed and grow in a healthy manner.

You must visit Chengdu to see the giant Panda Museum and research base. These adorable animals are found only in Sichuan province, and other nearby areas. The center spans over 90 acres and has many different rooms.

Langzhong

This small town is great if you are interested in seeing a different side to China. You'll find dozens of amazing sights in this black tiled town.

Emei Shan

Emei Shan offers history and spiritual relief. This mountain is one China's four most significant Buddhist mountains. The scene here is beautiful with its lush vegetation, fields and tea trees, flowering plants, and dozens of temples.

Kangding

Kangding, also called Dardo is the best place to visit if your goal is to learn more about Tibetan culture and not travel to Tibet. Beautiful Tibet lamaseries surround the town. This area is famous for the beautiful love song it inspired by its beauty.

This is where you can see the Anjue Temple built by the fifth Dalai Lama. The Nanwu Temple belongs to the Yellow Hat branch Tibetan Buddhism. You can experience the Walking Around the Mountain Festival on the eighth day, fourth lunar month.

Sichuan Province is an area in China that will leave you with amazing memories. It's a beautiful region with rich history, great food, and amazing people. You should not wait.

Sichuan - Tibet HWY, Sichuan Province

Tourists in China who wish to visit Tibet have made the Silk Road a favorite tourist destination. While there are several ways to accomplish this, it is increasingly popular to travel along the Southern Route.

This route covers 2140km and features some of the most beautiful scenery. There are wide open, lush valleys that are accented by tall, majestic mountains. These areas are home to some beautiful Tibetan villages as well as iconic yaks.

While the roads aren't in the best shape, they are improving. Warmer clothing is recommended. Also, be aware of side effects from high altitudes.

Here's a list of destinations you will stop at along the route.

Litang

This is the home of the seventh- and tenth Dalai Lama, and it also holds strong connections to Gesar Ling, the famous epic warrior. A town proudly boasts of this connection. You will be awestruck by the natural beauty of the area at an elevation of

4014m. You will find a friendly and relaxed atmosphere here. Additionally, visit the hotsprings and Qudenggabu for worshippers who spin prayer wheels and chant.

Shangri-La

Shangri-la, which is in North West Yunnan Province is on HWY Southern Route Sichuan-Tibet. This is where James Hilton found inspiration for The Lost Horizon, his British novel. This is where you can see the Ganden Sumtselling Monastery, a Tibetan monastery with a history of 300 years. The monastery houses approximately 600 Buddhist monks. There are many monasteries within Shangri-la. But this is the best. Guishan park has the most beautiful views and a temple. Visit this area between April and October to get the best views. The town closes at that time.

Batang

This small village is located 32km from Tibet. You can visit some amazing sites and the town is extremely friendly.

The Chode Gaden Pendeling Monastery, which is part of the Gelugpa branch of Buddhism, will be happy to show visitors around. There are many beautiful pieces of sculpture and old art throughout the monastery. If you're feeling adventurous, you can explore the various trails around town or visit the beautiful Tibetan villages high up in the hills.

Jiangsu Province

Jiangsu Province lies north of Shanghai and is home to a lush, green, fertile landscape. It is also one of the wealthiest regions in the country. This province is also known as "The land of fish and rice" because of its history of being rich off the East China Sea's waterways. As it descends from Tibet to Shanghai, the Yangzi River winds its way through the province. Cruising along Yangzi

River is a popular way for tourists to explore the region. This river offers stunning views of the countryside, as well as glimpses into traditional Chinese culture.

Suzhou

Marco Polo once described Suzhou's city as one of China's most beautiful (though he preferred Hangzhou). Suzhou was his first stop on his journey through China. It was full of beautiful whitewashed buildings, canals lined with trees and stunning gardens.

Suzhou is modern in every sense of that word. Suzhou's beauty lies hidden among the factories, skyscrapers or busy people. However, it is still there.

Suzhou is the oldest city in the Yangzi Basin. Suzhou's history spans over 2,500 years and it rose to great heights during Song dynasty. When it was connected the Grand Canal, it reached new heights. It thrived and was a major shipping and grain storage facility.

Suzhou had grown to the size it is today by the end the 12th Century.

Suzhou was one of the most prominent silk-producing cities in the country by the beginning of the 14th century. Famous and influential people from China made Suzhou their home. Suzhou flourished with its silk industry throughout the Ming-Qing periods. The Taiping Rebellion saw Suzhou taken by the rebels. In 1896 she opened her arms to foreign trade.

Suzhou's gardens are what draws people to it. You will find some of South Yangzi's most beautiful and oldest gardens. Although she originally had over 100 gardens, these numbers have fallen drastically. These gardens, however, are breath-taking and must see places.

Humble Administrator's Garden is a must-see for all visitors. It is the largest of the many gardens and is considered to be the most remarkable. It spans five hectares and was first established in the middle of the 1500's. It boasts many beautiful pavilions, lotus-ponds, bamboo woods, and winding bridges. This area is perfect for a stroll and to enjoy all that Suzhou has to provide.

Why not visit Lion's Grove Gardens just near Humble Administrator's Garden? In 1342, Tianru, the Buddhist monk founded it in memory of his master, Tianmu Mountain's Lion Cliff. When the gardens were completed, Ni Zan was a well-known artist. This garden is known for its many rocks named after lions. They are believed protect the Buddhist faith.

Suzhou has a lot to offer for cultural experience seekers. Twin Pagodas is a must-see attraction. They are seven stories tall and were built during the Northern Song period by applicants to imperial examinations, who wanted to show respect to their teachers.

Suzhou boasts many excellent museums. Suzhou Museum used to be the home of Taiping leader Li Xiucheng. It now houses beautiful maps and Qing dynasty stelae along with other interesting Chinese artifacts.

Suzhou Silk Museum, which is also famous for its silk industry, is a must-see. The museum contains fascinating information about the history of silk as well as beautiful examples. Also, you can witness silkworms at work chewing on mulberry leaves as well as spinning cocoons.

Kunqu Opera Museum makes a wonderful place to visit. Kunqu, the regional opera style, is located in a maze of narrow lanes. The museum has many wonderful photos and old costumes that you will enjoy. You might also see performances on the old stage. This is something that you must see.

The Temple of Mystery attracts visitors from all around the world. It is a Taoist temple which was established during the Jin Dynasty. However, it has been rebuilt several times. This is where you'll find the Three Purities Hall or Sanqing Dian, which is supported 60 pillars with gorgeous upturned eaves. This is Suzhou's only Song architecture, and it must not be missed.

Why not make a visit to Pan Gate This is Suzhou's original, coiled gate. It dates back to 1355. The elegant Wumen Bridge, which is arched and stretches along the canal, is a wonderful spot to stop, relax, and enjoy the natural beauty of Ruiguang Pagoda.

Suzhou is home to many beautiful attractions, such as lush gardens, stunning temples and museums, great restaurants, fascinating museums, and stunning scenery. You should not miss a trip to this place.

Lake Tai

It is not surprising that major television production firms have chosen Lake Tai for their backgrounds. Lake Tai's beauty is too incredible to describe. It is located near Wuxi and you can see the northern side of the lake as well as Turtle Head Isle. Lake Tai has a rich history and culture, making it very popular among tourists.

Lake Tai is surrounded on all sides by lush green rolling hills, sented tea gardens, and lush green tea fields. It's like a picture in a book. Chinese people travel here to find oddly shaped rocks they can use in their gardens. The rocks make Lake Tai stand out, making it charming. You'll soon discover why these rocks add an elegant touch to gardens.

The Brightness Pavilion, Guangming Tingn, is located at Turtle Head Isle's highest point. This is reached by following the path that runs north of Baojie Bridge. (Baojie Qiao) is located close to the southern entrance. This path will take you through stunning landscapes, and it is a feast both for the eyes and the senses.

You can shop at the many souvenir stalls located in the park's northern section and snap some pictures of the Perpetual Spring Bridge, also known as Changchun Qiao. To admire the lake's beauty, you can walk to the vantage spot and find a small pool. If all of this doesn't excite you enough, there is a ferry service that will take visitors to Sanshan. This island, also known as Three Hills Isle, was once home to pirates hundreds of years ago.

There are three amusement parks available. These are Tang Dynasty World. Three Kingdoms World. and Water Margin World. They are located on Turtle Head Isle's southern part. They were created to serve as the stage for period TV televisions that are based in historical literary pieces.

The accommodations are as serene and beautiful as their surroundings. Taihua Hotel is located at the top a hill and fully deserves its five star rating. The Lakeview Park Resort

Hotel may not be as luxurious as the former but it is still clean and comfortable.

Lake Tai has been a popular tourist location for many years. It is not hard to understand why. This lake has more than 90 island, historic sites, and spectacular scenery.

Gansu Province

Gansu Province has a long history of being part the legendary Silk Road. Over a thousand-years, merchants came from every corner of Asia, Central Asia, Europe, and beyond to trek through the deserts, mountains, and plains. They brought with them not only silk and other material, but also technology and religious ideas such as Buddhism.

Gansu is Northwest China's highlight; it houses Buddhist iconography as well as sculptures and temples.

Lanzhou

Lanzhou is the capital of the Province and is one the major cities along the Yellow River. It has been a significant garrison town for many centuries. There are so many amazing places to visit: the Gansu Province Museum is simply stunning with large displays of artifacts related to the region's past; White Cloud Temple is a magnificent Qing Dynasty Temple set in an idyllic setting; White Pagoda Hill, set in beautiful parks; and Lanshan Park.

Bingling Si

Bingling Si is a Buddhist grotto that survived into the modern era. It's located in the Liujiaxia Reservoir's isolated waters and has incredible examples ancient Buddhist sculptures. While the Magao Caves are one of the most popular Buddhist Caves in Dunhuang, they are not as well-known as the Bingling Si. However, they are still extremely rich.

Linxia

Linxia is a small community with a large personality. It is a wonderful place to explore and discover the beautiful region. You can also visit the Wanshou Temple and learn about the diverse ethnicities in the area.

Xiahe

This little town is nestled in the most beautiful setting - in a picturesque mountain valley. This is a wonderful place to get a feel for Tibetan culture, even if you cannot travel to Tibet. It is common to see Tibetan pilgrims in vibrant clothing. This is where you will feel like you are transported to another planet.

Mogao Caves

The Mogao Caves, which include almost 500 temples, are also known by the names Dunhuang Caves/Mogao Grottoes or the Caves of the Thousand Buddhas. They are located 25 kilometers southeast to Dunhuang in Gansu province. Mogao is literally "high up the desert", and some caves have a height of 50 meters.

The caves' oldest date back to 366 CE. These caves also have Buddhist art that dates back more than a thousand-years. Buddhist monks have used these caves for meditation for over a thousand years. The caves contain Buddhist sculptures or murals. They can hold statues up to 34m in height and smaller than 2 centimeters in width. Beautifully painted ceilings adorn the sidewalls.

Indian Buddhism is a major influence on the sculptures, especially those older. Paintings from artists from different dynasties are easily identifiable by their distinct styles and unique color schemes. With the discovery in the Library Cave of large numbers of scriptures, embroidery and other materials of the Tang Dynasty, it was possible to find a number of them. 17. It houses important paintings as well as woodblock printed texts such the Diamond Sutra. The Mogao Caves can also be used as a repository for various cultural exchanges over a millennium between China and other countries.

In summer, the caves are open from 8:30 am to 6:00 pm and in winter from 9:00am until 5:30pm. The vast cave network requires at least 3-4hrs to fully appreciate. Tourists are reminded that inside the caves, photography is not permitted.

Anhui Province

Anhui Province is often overlooked in favor of her richer neighbours, but it offers a slower way to experience authentic China. Hu Jintao's influence is a factor in her recent fortunes, but it has been a pleasure to meet the different ethnic groups that reside here.

Anhui is the Huizhou homeland. It's home to many beautiful traditional villages as well as mountainous landscapes that draw people like moths at a fire. The stunning scenery of Jiuhua Shan is where Buddhist monks offer prayers in gratitude to the souls for the deceased. Huang Shan is where you will find the highest peaks shrouded with misty white cloud.

Huangshan

Huangshan is a great destination for photographers looking for breathtaking scenery. Huangshan is also known as Yellow Mountains. This mountain range is found in the south of Anhui Province. It is famous for its unique mountain shapes, hot springs and sunsets. Tourists visit the Huangshan Sea of Clouds to view the breathtaking winter snow and beautiful views of the sky from the top.

The most popular peaks are: the Celestial Peak; the Bright Summit Peak; and the Lotus Peak. They are also the highest among the many mountains in the valley. Some of these mountains can reach more than 1,000 meters. There are many kinds of vegetation throughout the area. Huangshan is most well-known for its pine trees. Buddha's

Light, an unusual phenomenon of light that can be observed on selected days of the year, is also visible.

Huangshan, also known for being the sister mountain to the Jungfrau in Swiss Alps', is also a UNESCO World Heritage site. The captivating beauty of Huangshan makes it a popular theme in Chinese paintings, artworks, and art. During Qing and Tang dynasties, many thousand of poems were written about it.

Huangshan, as well many Huizhou villages from the past, offers tourists an insight into the culture and architecture. This area is known for its teahouses and Hui carvings. It also has a variety of Hui food, which is a must-see for all visitors.

Heilongjiang Province

Heilongjiang Province in China is the coldest part of China. Here temperatures can dip as low to minus 30°. Heilongjiang has some of its most famous tourist attractions, including the Ice Lantern Festival in winter.

Heilongjiang has more to offer than cold winters.

Haerbin

Haerbin is full of character. The city is bustling but also peaceful. Siberian Tiger Park is the main landmark. Here, the center studies and cares for Manchurian Tigers. The park is home to more than 100 Tigers, as well a pair African Lions and rare white Tigers.

Haerbin also has many other sights. Come here to visit the Daoliqu area and the Church of St. Sophia. The Stalin Park is another option. Sun Island Park is another. It is also worth visiting the Germ Warfare Base as well as the Seven-Tiered Buddhist Pagoda (the Temple of Bliss), the Temple of St. Sophia, the Confucius Temple, and Heilongjiang Museum. This will allow you to experience the Ice Lantern Festival in January/February.

Jingpo Hu

Jingpo Hu can be described as one of the most stunning places in northern China. There are many small islands scattered around the lake, as well as a shoreline lined with trees, scented flowers, and plants. The Diaoshuilou Waterfall lies near the lake. It is considered the place of dreams.

Qiqiha'er

Although not something most travelers would consider, this place is worth a visit. Before going to Zhalong Nature Reserve you can visit the Bukui Moorish Temple and Dacheng Temple. This reserve is a haven to over 260 bird species and is a heaven for bird-lovers.

Wudalian chill:

This was once a nature reserve but has been made into a volcano park which attracts tourists from Russia, China, and other international destinations. Longmen Stone Village has a lava pond that is stunningly beautiful. The Ice Caves can be visited to see Mother Nature at her best. Zhongling Temple offers the opportunity to visit several golden fat Buddhas.

Liaoning Province

China has some the most beautiful locations in the world. It is rich in tradition and culture and boasts beautiful natural landscapes. Liaoning is a remarkable spot in China.

A northern ethnic group called the Manchus was established as China's rulers during the 17th century. Some Westerners have given Liaoning the nickname Manchu Country.

Liaoning, the gateway to the beautiful northeast China region, is known as. It's home to numerous ethnic groups and is home to crumbling bridges, golden shores, borders to other nations, and a multitude of beautiful, colorful people.

Dalian

Dalian was recently voted China's most liveable city. You won't be disappointed with the many beaches and cultural attractions that make Dalian so attractive. It is worth noting Tiger Beach Park with its magnificent carved-marble statue of a protector tiger and amusement park, Bangchuidao Jingqu (5km from the city centre), and then the gorgeous pebbbly Fujiazhuang Beach (to the northwest).

You should next consider a trip to Dalian Modern Museum (Dalian Xiandai Bowuguan). It will be a great place to explore the rich history and culture in this wonderful region. You'll find the museum southwest of the city, near Xinghai Square.

Shenyang, which is the capital of the Province, is very proud of its long history. It became a Mongolian capital and trading center in the 11th century. However, it was later made the capital for the Manchu Empire just before the Qing Dynasty was founded. This city is fast and sprawling, especially considering that it houses approximately 6.5 millions people.

This beautiful city's most prominent attraction is the Imperial Palace. It was built by Nurachi, the Manchu ruler, and his song Huang Taiji.

The Pagoda of Buddhist Ashes ("Wugou Jingguang Sheli Ta") draws visitors like a moth at the flame. The brick pagoda, built in 1044, is located just a stones throw from the museum.

Dadong

The city, Dadong, is situated opposite Sinuji (North Korea). This area is popular for its view of North Korea. Although once there was a bridge linking the two countries, it was demolished by North Koreans during the Korean War. Dadong has a mix of

Japanese and Korean cultures, making it a truly unique place to explore.

Tiger Mountain Wall is part of the Great Wall of China. Most people don't realize it exists. It is located 25km to the north of the city. It is part of a wall the Ming constructed in the early days of their rule. It may be part the later design, but it still conjures up imagination.

The network of highways linking the major cities makes it easy to travel around Liaoning. It is possible to travel between the other parts of the province using buses and trains, making them an alternative to driving. Liaoning is a great place to get a glimpse at the incredible cultural and traditional heritage that the province has to offer.

Hunan Province

What can you say to summarize Hunan Province in one sentence? Fiery. This is China's home to the most spicy cuisines. It also houses the burning thoughts of Chairman Mao. He aimed to destroy China and the rest of the world by his beliefs. Today you'll find tourists reaching for tall glasses and wiping away the sweat as they gaze at the many effigies carved by Mao.

Although the tourism to Changsha is influenced by the Communist legacy, Hunan is much more than Mao. You can explore the quaint villages, bustling cities, and bustling towns of this vibrant region to your heart's desire. This is the best province for Chinese history and culture.

Changsha

This is the gateway into the home of Chairman Mao, Shaoshan. You can also explore many Mao cultural locations from here. Begin by visiting the Changsha City Museum, Hunan CPC Committee, and Hunan no.1 Teachers' Training School.

The Hunan Provincial Museum has a wealth of historical artifacts that can be viewed from many different periods. Yuelu Park or the Old City Walls can also be great places to explore.

Shashan

Only one reason to visit this village is the opportunity to discover the birthplace for Chairman Mao. To learn more about the man who changed the way the world views China, this town hosts over three million visitors each year. You can visit his Childhood School, Nanan School where his education was received, and the Museum of Comrade Mano before you go to Dripping Water Cave or Shao Peak.

Yueyang

This tea is so delicious that the Emperors requested it as a gift. This beautiful town sits on the Dongting Lake. The Yueyang Tower may be the most iconic landmark, but you will find many other attractions. For example, visit the Confucian Temple Par the Cishi Pagoda. Also, make sure to check out

Junshan Island. This is where the famous yinzhencha (silver needle tea) is grown.

Heng Shan

Heng Shan is one among the most beautiful spots in China. It is also the southernmost mountain of the five sacred Daoism mountains. Nanyue village is where you start the climb up the mountains. It has some sights to see. Although Wishing Harmong Peak is the highest peak, it takes four hours, but there are so many gardens, monasteries and temples on the mountain that it will take longer.

Hongjiang Old Town

If you are looking for authentic China, this historic town is where the Yuan River meets the Wu River. The Old Town is steeped in history with its old buildings and cobbled streets lined with red lanterns that bob in the wind. It is a maze of narrow lanes, but you will eventually find your way through to the Taiping Temple. The Money God Hall is also nearby.

Dehang

Dehang is a beautiful village located along the river. Here, the Miao (one the 56 officially recognized ethnicities in China) live. This is the perfect place to go for hiking, exploring the hills and valleys, as well getting to know Miao culture.

Jilin Province

Jilin Province was home to the Manchus. One of China's 56 recognized ethnic groups, they founded the Qing Dynasty. It is also the historical homeland of the Manchus. It became part the Japanese puppet country of Manchukuo only a few years later.

Jilin is also home of several other ethnicities including one million Koreans. It is therefore full of diverse architectural styles, languages and cultural attractions that make it a truly multicultural province.

Changchun

This was the Japanese capital for the puppet state of Japan between 1933-1945. It is now an industrial area. This city is home to the Puppet Empire's Palace and Exhibition Hall, which are two of its most well-known tourist attractions. This was Puyi's residence, the last Emperor from China. His reign ended on 11/11. The Japanese appointed him puppet emperor Manchukuo, and today you can tour his former residence to view the various quarters he and the lover were given.

Jilin City

Jilin City can be a beautiful place to visit in the winter when the needle-thin ice drops cover the trees of the riverfront. However, there is much more to the city; you can spend your time here. The Wen Miao temples are dedicated to Confucius. You will also find the Catholic Church and Century

Square. In January, the city also holds an Ice Lantern Festival, which is a must-see.

Changbei Shan

This is China's largest nature reserve, and it borders North Korea. Here you'll find breathtaking scenery, the Heaven Lake, and hot springs for relaxation. Spend a few hours exploring the Underground Forest and Changbei Shan Canyon.

Yanji

This is the capital and home of the Korean Autonomous Prefecture. It houses 80% Chinese Koreans. Here you can relax, get to know the Korean people and enjoy the diverse cuisines. There aren't any cultural attractions but the people here and the delicious food make up for it.

Ji'an

This Chinese city used to be part of the Korean Koguryo kingdom, which once ruled over large parts of northern China. The rich

Koguryo heritage was designated a World Heritage Site by UNESCO. Here you can visit The General's Tomb which is a 12-meter tall, pyramid-like monument designed for a 4th-century ruler.

You can also visit the Ji'an Museum or the Haotaiwangstelae. There are many other Koguryo sites you can explore. You won't be disappointed.

Xinjiang Province

Xinjiang (or New Frontier) is China's farthest province. For centuries, it has been a prized region by so many kingdoms. Xinjiang has been incorporated into China, but it remains a strong independent region.

This is not a part of China that can be called 'Chinese. Many people speak a totally different dialect of Chinese than in Beijing, and the food is completely different from what you'd find in Beijing.

Alaska is larger than Alaska. Many people see this province as a barren landscape. In reality, it is full of beauty and rich cultural history.

Urumqi

This is where the Silk Road's heritage can be sampled, although expect high-rise buildings to replace oasis tents with camels. There are many amazing places to visit. However, the Xingjiang Autonomous Region Museum has to be one of them! It cost $13 million to renovate this museum. The artifacts depict the history of the area and its significance in Chinese History.

Hongshan Park, and People's Park, are the main parks in the City. The former is a beautiful green oasis in urban chaos while the latter more of an amusement center. The center of Urumqi's Urumqi community is Erdaoqiao Market.

Tian Chi

Tian Chi lies at 2000m in Tian Shan Mountains. This beautiful lake is located just below the breathtaking Peak of God. This is where you can walk along trails that pass sheep and yaks or take a horseback ride to reach the top of the mountains. You can stay the night in one of the Kazakh-built yurts in summer.

Kuqa

Kuqa, a town that is both unusual and amazing to visit, is like a modern village with donkey-pulled carts. This used to be a place of refuge for merchants on the Silk Road. Kumarajiva also translated Buddhist scriptures into Chinese from Sanskrit.

There are plenty of things to do and sights to be seen. It is worth a visit to the Small Mosque first. After that, it is on to the Great Mosque which is just down the street. On Fridays, the bazaar will be open. You can also visit Qiuci Ancient City Ruins. These are the only remaining remnants of Qiuci.

There are many places you can visit in Xinjiang, a large province. Xinjiang has many attractions, including vibrant cities and charming towns. It is also home to proud villages.

Kashgaria Province

Xinjiang Province is a place of stark beauty contrasted with the shining beauty of places like Guilin. Although many consider this a desolated area, there is still beauty in the land and people. Kashharia was the name of the western Tarim Basin. This area is an important hub of the Silk Road. It also houses the Uighur heartland, which is one of China's most recognized ethnic groups.

Kashgar

Kashgar is the New Frontier's farthest point and considered to be the end of China. Chinese officials and diplomats visited Kashgar over 1000 years ago believing they had reached the ends of civilized civilization. In fact, Kashgar has been at the heart of many cultural struggles and cooperative efforts for hundreds of years.

Sunday Markets or Livestock Markets can be a great way to visit Kashgar. Learn the Uighur phrase, "Boish-Boish", which means "Coming Through!" This phrase is a warning to not move if you hear it. At dawn, it will be packed with farmers, traders, shepherds, and anyone else with bleating or naying animal.

Another wonderful place to visit is the Id Kah Mosque. The yellow-tiled mosque dates back from 1442. It can host up to 20,000 persons during celebrations or festivals. The Abakh Hoja Tob, where the ruler Abakh Hoja rests, is also accessible. He is believed to rest inside with his granddaughter Ikparham, also known as Xiang Fe (Fragrant Concubine), who was concubine of Qianlong Manchu Emperor Qianlong.

If you have time, visit the Kashgar Provincial Gallery, the Ha Noi Ruins, or the Mor Pagoda.

There are buses that run twice a week from this location to Kyrgyzstan. Make sure you have all paperwork completed before you cross.

Karakoram Hwy

The Karakoram Hwy links Pakistan through the Khunherab Pass. This highway has been used for centuries as a gateway by Silk Road merchants. Khunjerab Pass literally means "Valley of the Dead", a name that aptly describes the bandits who plunder the caravans, kill the traders and merchants, and then rob them of their wealth.

Even if the Karakoram Highway isn't something you want to do, it is worth a visit. The highway takes you through beautiful landscapes with Tajiks tending to yaks and camels in high-mountain meadows. Tashkurgan is your last stop on the journey.

Shanxi Province

Shanxi Province was once seen as an inhospitable region. It is situated between the ancient Chinese capitals (Chinese Capitals) and the grasslands of Inner Mongolia. This province has a beautiful landscape, friendly people, and a history that is as rich and diverse as the country.

Since ancient times, the province has been a centre of cultural exchange and commerce. Although it was subject to much destruction by generals fighting for power and glory over the centuries, the region also saw the rise in Buddhism philosophy. You won't find a more extensive collection of iconography and Buddhist temples anywhere else in China.

Taiyuan

This beautiful mix of the urban atmospheres of big Chinese cities with the slower pace of smaller towns is amazing. The Shanxi Museum, which ranks first among other provincial museums, is the best. The museum features many interesting displays of artifacts from different periods of Chinese history.

You will also find other great places here: the Chongshan Temple is a must-see, as well as the Shanxi Provincial Museum's Jinci Temple and Jinci Temple.

Pingyao

Pingyao feels small and transported back from the past. The village has remained unchanged in modernization, so it feels like it is still rooted in the Ming Dynasty. Its cobbled streets are swaying in a breeze and its red lanterns hang in the wind.

Take a stroll through the historic streets and buildings. There are many places to see, including the city walls, Rishengchang Financial House Museum Museum, county government offices, and Confucian Temple. The Shuanglin Temple is located outside the village walls.

Yuncheng

This area of rural Shanxi is a little-known gem. The Guan Yu Temple, the Bagua Tower and stunning views of surrounding countryside can be seen here.

Wutai Shan und Taihuai

This is China's sacred Buddhist mountainous region, home to Manjursi (the Bodhisattva Wisdom). The village at mountain's base is a small, charming place that can be used to start your climb to the peak.

There are many temples throughout the mountain. Tayuan Temples are Xiantong Temples. Nanshan Temples. Luohou Temples. Guangren Temples. Jinge Temple. A mountain trip will take you through some breathtaking scenery found throughout China.

Datong

Datong may be not the most picturesque town in Shanxi. However, it is rich with art.

Yuagang Caves is the most well-known landmark here. They are a group of grottos, which were established in around 480 CE. This is the first example of Buddhist artwork in China. Take the time to visit this site early in order to marvel at these stunning images.

Datong also features several other notable places to visit: the Huayan Temple and the Nine Dragon Screen, Shanhua Temple, Shanhua Temple, the Shanhua Temple, the Shanhua Temple, the Great Wall section, and the Shanhua Temple.

Zhejiang Province

Zhejiang Province lies south of Shanghai. It stretches along an uneven coastline towards Fujian Province. This region was rich because of its vast coastline and waterways.

Zhejiang, for lovers of culture, is not to be missed. Hangzhou, the provincial capital, is stunningly beautiful and offers relaxation, culture, inspiration, and beauty to all who visit. Visit the island of Putuoshan to see Guanyin, the Buddhist god of mercy.

Hangzhou

Hangzhou, the capital city of Zhejiang Province, is one of China's most iconic tourist destinations. Hangzhou, which has 6.16 million inhabitants, is located at the southern end, bordered by lush farmlands.

It has been a cultural and tourist center for hundreds of years, but its simple architecture and nondescript architecture make it hard to differentiate it from other major cities. People visit this place for the West Lake (Xi Hu), a perfect oasis within an urban jungle.

Marco Polo visited it in the 13th Century and called it "one of the most spectacular cities in the entire world." Hangzhou became extremely wealthy when it was connected to Grand Canal in 610CE. The city flourished by itself after the Jurchen (ancestors of Manchus) overthrew Song

Dynasty. Kaifeng was Kaifeng's capital during Song dynasty. However, the Jurchen invaded and forced the emperor to flee south. Hangzhou became their capital.

The Red Guards decimated much of the town in the Cultural Revolution. Even though some sites have been reconstructed, many of the old attractions are still available today.

Hangzhou's most popular attraction, West Lake, is something you should not miss. There are 36 lakes within China that can be called West Lake. But this is the most important and famous. The 8th century saw the creation of the lake after the governor cleared the marshy land. It was a picturesque spot that became famous over the years. There were pagodas built around it and causeways and islands were made. Gardens were also planted. Su Dongpo was a well-known poet who portrayed West Lake, a beautiful young lady whose beauty was enhanced through her striking gown.

Many attractions are available at West Lake. To enjoy stunning views of the ocean and the surrounding landscape, you can walk down to Su Causeway. Gu Hill is a great place to visit. It includes the Zhejiang provincial museum, Zhongshan Park. Seal Engravers Society. Quyuan Garden. Su Xiaoxiao is also on the list. She was a courtesan dating back to the 5th-century who died after she waited for her lover return. Legend has it that her ghost haunts this area.

The Mausoleum and Museum of General Yue Fi are another attraction that is popular with visitors. General Yue Fei (1103-42) was a commander among the southern Song armies. His character has been a favorite to be portrayed in opera, literature, and movies. He was the general that commanded successful campaigns against the invading Jurchen, but he was executed along with his son when the Song court returned and he was betrayed by Qin Hui, the perfidious Prime minister. He was exonerated in 1163 by Song Emperor Gao Zong and buried at his current place.

Inside the mausoleum, there is a large statue representing the general with an inscribed inscription: "Return our mountains and rivers". This is in reference to the invasion from the north by Jurchen.

Yellow Dragon Cave Park can also be a great place. It is located west from General Yue Fei's mausoleum. It is possible to reach a beautiful mountainside park by walking up a path just above the lake. This is a hidden gem, surrounded by bamboo forests and many ponds.

Continue up the path to find the yellow walled Baopu Taoist compound. It's named after Ge Hong (284-364CE). The sounds of chanting can still be heard in the mornings and evenings. Continue down the path and you will find the beautiful Baochu Pagoda of the 9th Century, which means Precious Pagoda.

You won't be disappointed if you love Chinese Temples. The Lingyin Temple is the Temple of the Soul's Recover. It was constructed in 326 CE. It has been rebuilt 16 times during the long years and is one of Hangzhou's most iconic attractions.

Hangzhou is worth a visit. It has stunning natural beauty, amazing museums, historical sites, restaurants, and hotels to fit every traveler's budget. This place will leave you feeling elated and never wanting to go home.

Exploring the Grand Canal Area

Exploring the Grand Canal area in Da Yunhe is like going back in history. With each village and town, you can see a different period in Chinese History. The Grand Canal is also an important part of this area.

China's economic and commercial growth has been enhanced by the Grand Canal. It is the longest human-made waterway that the Chinese have ever built. It was expanded during different dynasties, but finally became one during Sui Dynasty.

Suzhou

The Grand Canal's beginnings are in Suzhou. Take the number 11 bus to see the beautiful countryside as well as many of the charming water towns. Enjoy an unforgettable journey!

Precious Belt Ridge

Precious Belt Ridge is located about 4km south of Suzhou. This is where you will find the first stop when traveling down the Grand Canal. The name Precious Belt Ridge has a lovely story. It was named after Wang Zhongshu (a Tang Dynasty official). He sold his most prized possession, his leather belt, in order to raise enough money to build the bridge. It was built to great benefit people, so it was named after the official.

The bridge (Baodai Qiao), is made up of 53 arches and curves gracefully over the gentle, rippling rivers. It is loved by both fishermen and photographers for its peaceful atmosphere.

Lake Tai Area

Lake Tai is not only beautiful but also magical. You will fall in love with the region's natural beauty and charms, as well as the charming towns surrounding it. Dong Shan is a small island in the countryside. It is the home of Zijin'an, the Purple Gold Nunnery. The nuns live peacefully in seclusion.

Tianping Shan, a place you should visit if your passion is nature or hiking, is Tianping Shan. It is a lush, low-populated region. It is beautiful and has healing properties. Ideal for tired feet!

Lingyan Shan can be found approximately 11km southwest Suzhou. It is also called the "cliffe of the spirits". While it's now a Buddhist monastery, the area was once home the palace in which Emperor Qianlong resided. Unfortunately, the Taipings destroyed the building in the 19th-century. The atmosphere is peaceful and beautiful today.

Tongli

Tongli canal town, which retains its authentic architecture and tranquil atmosphere, is a popular daytrip destination from Suzhou. Tongli, which was established in the 9thcentury, meets all expectations for a charming town.

Walking the Old Town can be an enjoyable activity. Walking along the canals can be half the fun. The other half is to attempt to find your path back. Along the way, you'll be able to admire the beauty of traditional buildings and hear the soft rippling sounds from the canal.

Tongli is a beautiful place to visit. Gengle Tang is a vast estate that dates back the Ming Dynasty. It is home to 52 halls, which will delight the eyes and inspire your imagination.

The Pearl Pagoda is located in the northern section of town. It dates back the Qing Dynasty. Despite having been restored recently, its original charms were not diminished.

The Tuisi Garden is one of the most spectacular attractions in the town. It fits the title that means'retire, contemplate'. You are now ready to experience the Chinese Sex Culture Museum, which will relax your mind and body. Everything you need to know about sex and China in China can be found here, from the interesting to the absurd to the sad.

Mudu

Mudu is known for its beautiful gardens. It was established in the Ming Dynasty. This town offers a more authentic flavor of old China than its neighbours.

It's like traveling through each era in Chinese history by exploring the Grand Canal. You'll be amazed by the vibrant history, incredible attractions, and the warmhearted hospitality of the people. Every step you make along the Grand Canal leads you closer and closer to China's people.

Yunnan Province

Yunnan Province is a part of China you may not have known existed. It is home to some amazing scenery and is one the most picturesque in East Asia. The south is filled with tropical rainforests while the north is covered in snow-capped mountain peaks.

The scenery isn't all that diverse. Yunnan's population has almost half its inhabitants from different ethnicities. It is far removed from Beijing and other areas along the east coast influenced by Han Chinese.

Yunnan in China is the place you'll never believe until it's actually there. So, what are you waiting?

Kunming

Kunming is located in central Yunnan. It's a vibrant modern Chinese city with fascinating glimpses of its 2000-year-old past. It was a remote outpost before the Nanzhao Kingdom captured it and made the city a second capital. It became once again a Chinese settlement after the Mongols took over.

The Yunnan Provincial Museum features some of the oldest bronze bells from the region. This museum also offers an opportunity to see amazing Buddhist art and learn more about the diverse ethnic cultures within the region. It's worth visiting the Tang Dynasty Pagodaas West Pagoda as well East Pagoda and East Pagoda of the Tang

Dynasty Pagodaas. Also, Yuantong Temple is a great place to visit. This temple is more that a thousand year old.

Other places worth visiting include the Kunming City Museum. The peaceful Green Lake Park is another place to visit. And the many mosques of the city, including the Nancheng Mosque which is the oldest.

Dian Chi

Dian Chi is a lake located to the south-east of Kunming. It is home to a variety of hamlets belonging different minorities. The Yunnan Nationalities Museum, Xi Shan, and Grand View Park are also available here.

Shilin

This is a unique location that draws many visitors. It's a group of limestone pillars. According to legend, it was where immortals built a temple out a mountain for lovers seeking privacy. These trails offer some amazing hiking opportunities.

Dali

Is it Dali oder Lijian This is the question you will continue to ask yourself. Lijian might be the prettiest, but Dali can definitely hold her own. This small town is amazing, home to the Bai ethnic tribe that established the Nanzhao kingdom back in the 8thcentury.

Dali offers many wonderful attractions. The Three Pagodas, which are the city's most famous landmark, should be seen. But the Dali Museum should also not be missed. You should visit Erhai Hu, the Erhai Lake (there are many markets in the vicinity).

Other Famous Locations

China also offers many more tourist attractions than the ones listed above. These are other places that you should visit during your trip to China.

1) Li River - This is a river that flows through the Guangxi Zihuang area of China. It originates from the Mao'er Mountains.

Tourists to this region must not miss the Li River Cruise.

2) Summer Palace - It is 15 kilometers north of Beijing in the Haidian District. It boasts stunning lake views and is China's largest royal parks. It is also a UNESCO World Heritage listed site.

3) Giant Wild Goose Pagoda - This Buddhist pagoda is 64 meters high and can be found in Xi'an province, Shaanxi Province. It contains many Buddha figurines and sutras. They were brought here from India.

Jiuzhaigou (or Jiuzhaigou): This valley lies on the Tibetan Plateau's e.ge and is well-known for its waterfalls as well as its lakes. It is also a UNESCO World Biosphere Reserve and a national park.

The Best Time To Visit

China is spread across a huge area. It can be extremely hot or cold, depending on the season. Prepare for whatever Mother Nature throws at your face.

However, you should consider visiting China during the spring or autumn. These seasons are especially pleasant in most of China. Due to the peak tourist season, summer is not as busy. You won't see as many tourists during this time. Accommodation will be more affordable and easier to find, as well as better views of all tourist sites.

It is also a good idea to avoid public holidays such the Chinese New Year, May Day Holiday and the Chinese New Year. These holidays are marked by large groups of Chinese people taking small family vacations. You will have difficulty finding affordable accommodation or train tickets.

Chapter 4: Chinese Food You Should Try

China is a huge country that is almost as large as the United States. China is a mixture of different ancient empires, civilizations, and there is a significant cultural diversity that is not found in the US. Although not as diverse in culture as India, China's food is quite diverse. The country is also home to many different cuisines. All of it will likely fall under the category of Chinese food to untrained foreign eyes. However, once you try the food, you will be surprised at the subtle differences.

Eight principal Chinese food traditions are included. These traditions are called the "Great Traditions" because they include four:

1) Jiangsu. This is also known Huiayang. Jiangsu cuisine or Huiayang cuisine is generally very mild. The savory food also tends to have a slight sweetness. Jiangsu food is more subtle and delicate than other Chinese cuisines that are more fiery in their

flavours. The majority of food that can be incorporated into this cuisine is not spicy. This makes it great for West-based people who aren't accustomed to spicy foods. As with many Chinese dishes, the base of these dishes is meat with a heavy emphasis on pork. Jiangsu traditions include seafood, including freshwater fish and shellfish. Jiangsu cuisine is well-known for its variety of breakfast options. These breakfast options include steaming dumplings made out of crab. Jiangsu is typically available in major cities in South China. However certain Northern Chinese cities may also have Jiangsu restaurants that are marked.

2) Cantonese, the Chinese cuisine most known in the west. Cantonese cuisine makes up the majority of "Chinese food" in the West. Western tourists should make sure to look for Cantonese dishes if they wish to eat familiar Chinese foods. Cantonese food is more mild than Jiangsu but contains a lot more spice. One major

difference you'll notice between these two branches is that Cantonese cuisine leans more towards the salty side than Jiangsu. The Cantonese subcategory is Chinese cuisine and all three meals feature interesting dishes. But the highlights of this traditional are the small snacks served as appetizers with larger meals. These are also called Dim Sum. Even though you are familiar with Cantonese cuisine, don't forget that Cantonese cuisine is more adventurous that other Chinese food styles. This is due to the way the meat is prepared. Don't be alarmed if you accidentally eat unusual meats. Although certain Cantonese recipes contain meats that look like snakes or dogs, these dishes can be expensive and difficult to avoid.

3) Shandong. This Chinese cuisine is perhaps the most authentic you'll find. Although most other Chinese food traditions can be influenced in some way by foreign influences, such as the introduction of

chicken or beef, Shandong cooking is still grounded in ancient traditions. Find Shandong restaurants to enjoy authentic Chinese cuisine. Shandong cuisine uses a variety of meats that aren't standard, including prawns (crabs), crabs, scallops, and squid. Surprisingly, Shandong is perhaps the oldest and most unaltered Chinese cuisine. However, no Shandong dish contains pork. This is unusual for Chinese cuisine since pork is a popular meat in China.

Sichuan: Sichuan food is perhaps the opposite of Jiangsu. Sichuan cuisine can be described as spicy and blisteringly spicy. Jiangsu cuisine can be mild and sweet. Sichuan cuisine is often described as being so spicy your mouth will burn! It may seem like Sichuan cuisine has a lot of chili peppers. However, this is not the case. Sichuan cuisine includes a Chinese spice called Sichuan peppercorn. This peppercorn adds a distinctive flavor to dishes prepared in Sichuan cuisine. This is the key difference between Northern Chinese and Southern Chinese cuisines. Chongqing also has a large population that eats Sichuan cuisine. Sichuan and Chongqing may not be the best places to taste Sichuan cuisine. Instead, you should look for areas with migrant workers. Sichuan cuisine, although considered high-end food by Chongqing and its home town, is considered budget food in other cities. This is due to the fact that most Chinese people can't handle it. Ironically, Sichuan food that is lower end can often be more tasty than its expensive, sterilized counterpart. For a truly memorable culinary experience, take a chance to visit large cities with many migrants.

While not as well-known and widely known as the Great Traditions of China, the other four Chinese customs are worth your time. Here are the four less well-known Chinese culinary traditions:

1) Fujian. While Fujian cuisine might not be well-known outside China it is famous within China. Fujian cuisine uses meats and other vegetables from the sea, its many estuaries, as well as their coats. The Chinese consider it one of 8 Chinese food traditions that is the best. This flavor is enhanced through the variety of cooking methods used by Fujian chefs. Special emphasis is also given to the natural broth. The legends that surround Fujian food are numerous. However, the most significant one relating to this type of Chinese cuisine is the story about a Buddhist monk. Buddhist monks and especially Buddhist monks vow to live a vegetarian life because they believe all of life is sacred. According to legend, a Buddhist monk in Fujian, who was living in a monastery, became so excited by the smells and flavors of Fujian cuisine that he decided to jump the monastery wall to have some. It's clear that one of the world's most disciplined people couldn't resist the lure of

Fujian cuisine. A trip to China is well worth it!

2) Zhejiang. Zhejiang's most notable feature is its ability to produce the most liquid Chinese food in the world. Most Zhejiang cuisines are soups or soup variations, which may make the Chinese food tradition seem a bit tedious. Zhejiang soups are delicious and offer a surprising variety of flavours. Zhejiang cuisine has a light flavor and a similar flavour to Jiangsu's Northern dishes. Zheijang foods tend to be sweeter than others, or slightly sweeter than the other end of the food spectrum. There is also a hint Chinese tangy sourness added to help even things out. Zheijang is a Chinese cuisine that focuses on either meat or vegetables. However, it's unique in that it incorporates both elements to make a unique experience. Zheijang cuisine can usually be found in Hangzhou or Ningbo.

Hunan: Hunan is an Asian cuisine that may be familiar even though you have never tried it. Hunan is frequently featured in Kung Fu films. In many ways, the Chinese Kung Fu film's name dish packs just as much punch. Since they are not "Great" foods, it is reasonable to assume that these cuisines may be less popular than their "greater". This would make it fair to assume these cuisines may be more thrilling than their "great" counterparts. This is true especially for Hunan food. Hunan is the best choice for those who want to try Sichuan food, but are looking for more spicier options. Sichuan cuisine might be considered borderline masochistic. However, Hunan cuisine could be considered almost fatal. Hunan cuisine can also be considered extreme Sichuan food. Hunan cuisine offers a unique experience unlike any other.

4) Anhui. Anhui cuisine is one of China's more traditional food traditions. Anhui cuisine can be a wonderful choice if your goal is to have an authentic experience and/or practice Orthodoxy. Anhui cuisine

can be described as a extreme version or Sichuan cuisine. Hunan is one example of extreme Sichuan cuisine. Anhui cuisine is a way to bring the Shandong's rustic elements to a new level. Anhui food uses wild herbs and is prepared in traditional cooking methods. Anhui food is almost exclusively prepared using oil. However, traditional Anhui cooking uses water-based methods like steaming and boiling. This may give the impression that Anhui cuisine is more bland than it actually is. Anhui's wild herbs are well-known for their power and can be used by experts to create new flavours that will blow your mind. There are three more branches to Chinese cuisine in Anhui. These three sub branches are: the Yangtze Anhui is located around Yangtze River, Huai Anhui is located around Huai River, as well as the Southern Anhui. They are all found in the southern half Anhui province. These Anhui culinary subdivisions differ in subtle ways. The differences are mostly due to how different types of hers are used for flavoring the food. I recommend trying all three types Anhui food!

Other than these 8 traditional Chinese food dishes, 4 great traditions, and 4 lesser-known, there are many other branches in Chinese cuisine. These branches are often heavily localized and combine well-established Chinese cuisine traditions. These branches are Chinese cuisine.

1) Shanghai: Shanghai is a cuisine that isn't often considered to be part of Chinese food. China's second-largest city and most vibrant is Shanghai. People all across the country travel to Shanghai to make their fortunes. This allows for a lot more intermingling of the Northern and Southern Chinese cultures. It was a result that Northern and Southern food traditions began to merge. This led to the creation of Shanghai cuisine. It often has the best of both Sichuan and Jiangsu cuisines. Imagine something spicy but not hot enough to make you feel sick, while being tangy yet sweet. This is truly a

unique combination. It's no surprise that Shanghai food is so popular in China. It is interesting to note that this particular Chinese cuisine style has inspired ramen, a convenient food that is very popular with college students and avid gamers.

2) Chaozou: This cuisine is also known to be Teochew. It originates in Guangdou. Chaozou's unique flavor is due to the unique cultural makeup in Shantou. Chaozou cuisine can often be compared to other East Asian cuisines, such as Thailand or Vietnam. Chaozou has been greatly influenced, and has experienced significant growth in Hong Kong. Chaozou food is very different to other Chinese cuisines, in particular because it lacks soups. If you are visiting Hong Kong, Chaozou cuisine is worth a try. It is perhaps the most famous Chaozou dish and is often considered to rival the Peking duck. Chaozou fishballs can be substituted for duck if you're not hungry, but make sure

you enjoy the Chaozou dessert made out of yam past! It's a must-try!

3) Guizhou. Guizhou cuisine is one more example of the emerging cuisines created by the movement of Chinese people from North-South. It is very similar to Sichuan food, but much milder. Guizhou cuisine tends not to be as fiery and spicy as Sichuan cuisine. Guizhou dishes have this unique flavor because they use a special vegetable called the zhergen. Although zhergen is a root plant, it is very similar to carrot. However, this is where the similarities end. Zhergen's unique flavor can only be described by peppery, with a slight hint of sourness. Guizhou cuisine gets its unique flavor from zhergen. You must try the Sour Fish Hotpot if you're dining in Guizhou. The delicious taste of this dish will make you want to return time and again. If you try it once, you will want to make it at least three more times before it is gone!

4) Beijing. Beijing cuisine has been compared to Hong Kong's. Although the braised duck originated in Hong Kong's Chaozou traditions, Beijingers proudly claim they created it long before Hong Kong. This dish is also known as the Peking Duck. Peking duck is a famous Chinese dish that has been featured in many films. Beijing is worth a visit. It's delicious and well-worth the effort. Beijing cuisine has very little to offer, except for the Peking Duck. The street food of Shanghai and Hong Kong is not as amazing as Beijing's. They do have decent noodles, freshly baked buns, pickles inspired by Pakistan, and fresh noodles. Beijing is a city with few frills. The Peking duck however is an exception and well worth a trip to China's capital.

5) Imperial: Explore the high-end areas of Beijing, and you'll find an entirely different kind of food. There are many restaurants in this area that charge outrageous prices, but it's worth it if your budget can bear the cost.

Imperial cuisine is an imposing name that deserves to be remembered for the richness of its ingredients. Cixi, the Dowager Empress of China, was famous for demanding exotic food from her cooks during the Qing Dynasty. Ingredients such as the paws from Bactrian camels and the fins off sharks were used in this food. It was food discovered at frontiers of Qing Empire expansion. These food are extremely rare and expensive. But if you're a person who loves adventure, then this food might be for you. Beijing Imperial cuisine's story is what makes it so special. This adds an air of wonder to the cuisine, and gives it a sense of history. Imperial cuisine goes beyond just being a delicious meal.

In China, many major cities also offer Western food like burgers and pizzas. You can find many international brands in China, including McDonalds, KFC and Pizza Hut. Also, you should try Chinese street food on your trip! Although Chinese street food may not be as well-received or as authentic as those of the major cuisines it is delicious nonetheless. It is quick and easy to prepare, so it's a great choice for those who are walking or exploring Beijing or Shanghai.

Chapter 5: Beijing - Capital China

Beijing is not only China's capital, but it also serves as the country's hub for international trade, educational, political, and cultural activities. It is located north of China. It is close to Tianjin and is therefore one of the largest ports of entry.

Beijing is also included in China's six ancient capitals. It is the centre of both China's politics, as well as its society throughout history. Beijing is now a main destination for tourists who are interested to see the ancient past, as well as the current development of China.

Beijing has become a tourist hot spot, with more than 4 million international tourists and over 140 million Chinese tourists per year.

January 2013: Passport holders of 51 countries were granted a visa free stay of up 3 days when they make an international transfer through Capital Airport. These passport holders come from the United States of America.

Beijing's Top Ten Attractions

Great Wall in Beijing: Beijing is China's political center. Beijing is also the country's most strategic city. Beijing's Great Wall has been built by many dynasties. Beijing's Great Wall was constructed during the Ming Dynasty in 1368-1644. It is the longest preserved wall and most visited, covering more than 560 kilometers (342 miles). It has 827 platforms, innumerable towers and 71 passes. The Huanghuacheng is home to the Badaling, Mutianyu and Gubeikou sections.

Tiananmen Plaza - This square is at the center of the city, near the Chang'an Avenue's Midpoint. This is where tourists can watch the national flag being raised for the country. It also houses other important destinations like the Monument to the People's Heroes (also known as the

Chairman Mao Zedong Memorial Hall), the Great Hall of the People and the Tiananmen Tower. This Square attracts many visitors from all walks of Beijing, so it is a must-see spot.

Forbidden Citadel - Also known to be the Palace Museum. It is located in central Beijing. Gu Gong is its Chinese name. It was the royal palace that 24 emperors occupied during the dynasties Ming-Qing. According to ancient Chinese Astronomers, the Polaris (or the Purple Star) was found in the heaven's center. The Purple Palace is where the Heavenly King lived. They believed the Purple City was the name of an emperor's palace. It was only allowed if the emperor granted it permission. The palace's name was changed to "The Purple Forbidden City," and it is now also known as "The Forbidden City", or the "Palace Museum."

Summer Palace - The Haidian District is north of Beijing. It is located 15 kilometers from Beijing's city center. Summer Palace is

China's oldest and most preserved royal park. It showcases Chinese landscape and horticulture through cultural activities and breathtaking natural views. It is also known for being the "museum royal gardens."

National Stadium - Also known under the Bird's Nest name, this stadium can be found in Chaoyang District. It is part the Olympic Green Village. It was designed to be the main venue for the 2008 Beijing Olympic Games. The National Stadium is where many Olympic events were held, including weight throw and track and fields. The National Stadium was opened for tourists in 2008 after the Olympics. It is now the main area for both national and international sporting competitions and other recreational activities. Here will be the opening ceremony and closing ceremony of the Winter Olympic Games 2022.

Temple of Heaven- Located in Chongwen District. This is where the Heaven Worship Ceremony of the Qing, Ming, and Qing emperors was held. The Temple of Heaven, an old sacrificial temple, is still the country's largest architectural masterpiece. The park was first opened to the general public in 1988. It is a showcase for ancient philosophy, religion, as well as philosophy. Its grand architecture takes you back to the ancient Eastern civilization.

Ming Tombs – Located in the 50-kilometer northwest of Beijing, at the foot Tianshou Mountain are the Ming Tombs. Here you will find the mausoleums 13 emperors from Ming Dynasty. The Thirteen Tombs in Ming Dynasty are also called this place. This is where the most famous emperors are buried. Every year, visitors and locals flock to this area to marvel at its beautiful architecture and to learn about its mysterious history.

Beijing Zoo – The Beijing Zoo is a unique zoo that opened in China. It is located in the Xicheng District. It boasts an impressive collection of animals, several historic sites, as well as a variety of exhibition halls. The zoo is home to approximately 450 animals of different species, and has at least 5,000. Visitors spend most of their time in the zoo viewing wild and rare animals from China. This includes giant pandas of gold, north-east tigers, milos, and miludeer. American bison, Polar bears, Kangaroos and Zebras, as well as elephants and giraffes are all available.

Beijing Hutong -- The Beijing Hutong and Courtyards culture is the most authentic Beijing culture. This is because they can attract more tourists to Beijing than large mansions and high rise buildings. Hutong comes from Mongolia and means water well. It is also the name of a narrow street or lane measuring approximately 30 feet by 30 feet. Hutong is today made up of many streets, lanes and alleyways that are representative of local culture.

Yonghe Lamasery – Also known by the Harmony and Peace Palace Lamasery. This perfectly preserved lamasery is found in the city's northeast corner. It is China's largest lamasery. It was the residence of Prince Yongzheng in the past, before he became an emperor. The Qing Dynasty converted the residence to a lamasery in 1744. It was thus made the national centre of the Lama administration.

Chapter 6: Chengdu – Capital of Sichuan Province

Chengdu, also called the "Heavenly State", serves as Sichuan Province's capital. It is located at the centre of Chengdu Plain. Chengu, which is home to giant pandas, covers an area approximately 4,749 mile. It is home to over 11 million people.

Chengdu is known for its abundance of natural resources. In Chinese, it's called "Tian Fu Zhi Guo". The city boasts fertile lands with abundant mineral resources. It has the Dujiangyan Irrigation Project that covers over 700 kilometers. The project produces about 150 to 180,000,000 kilowatts (or water) of water. The irrigation is supplied by the Tuo and Min Rivers, both branches of Yangtze River.

Chengdu's Top 10 Attractions

Chengdu Panda Breeding and Research Center. The giant pandas, which are beloved by both locals and foreigners alike, are considered one of China's most precious national treasures. They are found in Sichuan, Gansu, and Shaanxi provinces. China has fewer than 1000 giant pandas. Around 80% of the giant pandas live in the Sichuan province. The Sichuan Province is the most popular destination for giant pandas. The Chengdu Panda Breeding and Research Center has activities related to giant pandas. Because of the Shaanxi Rare Animal Rescue and Breeding Center incident where two giant pandas died from canine dystemper, close contact with them is now prohibited. Visitors are prohibited from touching a panda or taking part in the volunteer programs.

Wuhou Temple is a temple located in Chengdu's southern suburb. It is dedicated Memorial Temple of Marquis Wu), Zhuge Luang, the Wuhou and Marquis Wu of Shu Kingdom. Built next to the Liu Bei shrine, the temple measures approximately 37,000 sq. meters. Liu Bei was the ruler of Shu. The Wuhou Temple, which was originally part of the Liu Bei temple, was integrated into the Liu Bei temple at the beginning the Ming Dynasty. The temple is surrounded by classic red walls which make it nostalgic. It also contains old cypresses.

Jinli Street: Located just east from the Wuhou Temple, you will find the Jinli Street. Here, you can enjoy Chengdu's relaxing atmosphere. The history shows that the Jinli Street used to be the most popular location for baldachin (ornate cloth). It was also one the busiest commercial areas, especially during Shu Kingdom (221-223). It was then renamed the "First Street of the Shu Kingdom." The Jinli Street was opened to the public in October 2004. It is now one of China's most visited places. Both locals as well as tourists visit this area to unwind, enjoy unique local foods, and admire traditional-style buildings.

Chunxi Road: This pedestrian street has been compared to Paris' Eiffel Tower. It is where most people visit when they are in Chengdu. To shop in Chengdu's fashion center, first-time travelers to Chengdu will visit the Chunxi Road Pedestrian St. It is located within the Jinjiang District. It measures approximately 200,000 sq. meters. It connects the East Street and Mercantile Corporation. Today, in addition to being a fashion hub, you will find tasty snacks from all over the nation.

Sichuan Museum – Sichuan Museum - Southwest China's largest comprehensive museum is located in west Chengdu City. It is just beside the famous Huanhua Stream

Park. Sichuan's nickname "The Land of Abundance", is a proud one. It has lots to offer in the way of natural resources. Also, its culture is rich and has a long history. Sichuan Museum is home to all the province's collections. It is not surprising that it is China's top museum. It houses 260,000 pieces, including 60,000 historic relics. Of these, 1,399 are unrivaled in the entire world. This huge collection can be found on an area of around 12,900 m2, and further divided into 14 exhibitions halls. The museum also regularly hosts rare exhibits.

Sichuan Museum -- This museum is the most comprehensive in southwest China. It is located near Huanhua Stream Park which is west Chengdu. The museum showcases Sichuan's historical collection, which is a testament to the province's strong cultural heritage and abundance of natural resources. Sichuan Museum houses 14 exhibition halls housing 260,000 objects. It contains more than 60,000. 1,399 unmatched historical relics.

Wide and narrow Alley - This tourist area is part the Chengdu Cultural and Historical Reserves, which also includes the Wenshu Monastery (and Daci Temple) reserves. It comprises Narrow Alley, Wide Alley, and Well Alley. These alleys are an ancient city and contain 45 courtyards. The Chengdu history is represented by the Wide- and Narrow Alley.

Three-Star Piles Museum- Also known as Sanxingdui Museum. It covers an area approximately 40 kilometers. Its total exhibition area measures approximately 4,000 sq. meters. This museum is located northeast of Three-Star Piles archaeological site and west of Guangchan. It has items about China's archeology.

Dujiangyan Irrigation Project is a world-famous no-dam irrigation project. It is also the oldest. It is also known as one of China's greatest achievements in science development. This project is composed three parts, Feishayan; Baopingkou; and Yuzui. All are designed to automatically control the water flow from mountains to plains.

Mt. Qingcheng, a mountain in the southwest of Sichuan Province. It is one among the most popular Taoist mountain in the country. It is surrounded by lush, deep-green trees. It is also surrounded on all sides by many peaks. Mt. Qingcheng can be described as a "most tranquil and peaceful mountain in the world."

Jiuzhai Valley National Park (north of Chengdu City) - This national park is found in Nanping County. Because of its breathtaking scenery, the Jiuzhai Valley has been referred to as a "wonderland" by both locals and tourists. For Tibetans, the valley is both a sacred mountain and a watercourse.

Chapter 7: Guilin - City of Stunning Landscape

Guilin is located northeast of South China in GuangxiZhuang Autonomous Regional's GuangxiZhuang. It is often called the country's Pearl because of its flourishing tourist industry. It is approximately 10.734 miles in area, but it is much smaller than some other tourist cities in China. Guilin's beauty is what attracts tourists to the city. Its hills are oddly-shaped; its rich vegetation includes bamboos and conifers; its water is clear and crystal clear; and the caves are amazing-formed. Guilin is also a cultural center due to its over 2,000 year history. Guangxi is also its center for political, economic, and cultural affairs.

Guilin's top 10 Attractions

Li River Cruise - This is the highlight on any northeastern Guangxi Provincial trip. The Li River runs from Guilin and Yangshuo. As you cruise down the clear waters of the river, you'll see incredible Karst peaks. You will see water buffalo in the fields. Schoolchildren and fishermen are riding bamboo rafts. A few peasants can also be seen planting rice pads. The stunning scenery along the Li River is why it is so popular among tourists in China.

Reed Flute Cave, 5 km north of Guilin Downtown. The cave's name comes from its growing verdant vegetation, which makes people fluent. The cave is water-eroded and has impressive stone pillars, columns, and stalactites. It also contains rock formations that result from carbonate deposit. The cave is 240 m long and features colored lighting.

Elephant Trunk Hill — Also known by Xiangbishand this hill can be found on the Li River's western banks. Its shape resembles an elephant that drinks water from river using its trunk. Between the hill's legs and trunk is the Water Moon Cave, a semi-round cave through which water penetrates. You can see the reflection of the water in the cave, which will resemble a full moon. This is what makes the hill special. There are also laudatory inscriptions found on the cave's wall.

Folded Brocade Hill – Also known as Diecai Hill or the Diecai Hill. This hill is located in northeast Guilin and is one of the most visited tourist spots. It is famous for its spectacular scenery and exquisite stone carvings. The Folded Brocade Hill rocks look similar to textiles or cloths, which are piled up against each other. The hill is also known by other names, such as the Wind Cave Hill and the Laurel Hill. These are derived from the laurels which are scattered along its slopes.

Yangshuo: This county is located northeast of GuangxiZhuang Autonomous Regional and southeast of Guilin. The region is blessed with the beautiful Li River that runs through it. Yangshou is often referred to as one of China's most beautiful provinces. Guilin's most beautiful spot is Yangshou.

Yangshuo marks the end of the cruise along Li River.

Seven Stars Park, Guilin City's largest comprehensive park, is located on Guilin City's east bank. The park's seven peaks of the Crescent Mountain (the Putuo Mountain) are the reason it is so named. The Big Dipper constellation is also represented by the peaks. Clear water, deep canyons, beautiful mountains, stone forest and cultural relics make up the Seven Star Park. It also contains a large number of animals and plants. The main attractions include the Seven Stars Cave (Crescent Mountain), the Flower Bridge and the Light of China Square.

Two Rivers, Four Lakes Scenic Spot: This tourist attraction is located in Guilin. It contains the Peach Blossom River (Taohua), Li River and the Ronghu Lake. It is divided into ronghu–Shanhu Lake Scenic Area and Guihu Lake Scenic Area. These areas feature beautiful ecological landscapes and reflect the city's culture.

Jingjiang Prince City Scenic Area. This area is around the Solitary Beauty Peak. It is an important tourist destination, built in the exact spot where Prince Jingjang from the Ming Dynasty lived. The man-made sites are beautiful and blend well with the natural beauty of this area. It features Guilin's rich history and culture.

Wave-Subduing Hill (located above Li River's west bank and 1.24 miles away from Elephant Trunk Hill) It is also known under the Fubo Hill. It is one of Guilin's most picturesque spots. Wave-Subduing Hills is 698.8 feet tall and stands 203.4 feet above sea level. Half the hill is located on land and the other in the river. Because the water is blocked and whirlpooled against the hill, it generates powerful subduing wave. There will be stalactites, natural rock formations, pavilions and artificial cloisters. These are some of the unique features that make the hill special. The hill's foot is home to the Thousand-Buddha Cave, the Sword-Testing Rock, the Pearl-Returning Cave and Sword-Testing Rock.

Dragon's Backbone Rice Terraces (Southeast of Longsheng County) - The Dragon's Backbone Rice Terraces, which are considered the most impressive terrace in China, is located to the southeast. It is a huge area of rice terraces which extends in layers around the summit. It was constructed during Yuan Dynasty. The Zhuang people are known for their hard work and outstanding wisdom.

Chapter 8: Hangzhou - Heaven on Earth

Hangzhou is at the center of Zhejiang Province's political, cultural, economic affairs. It is located at the Qiantang River's lower reaches in southeast China, and approximately 180 kilometers from Shanghai. It is known as the Grand Canal's southern terminus.

Hangzhou's subtropical Monsoon climate is what makes it a popular tourist destination throughout the year.

Hangzhou's West Lake is the most prominent landmark. This is because of its breathtaking natural beauty, which blends well into most of the city's cultural and historic sites. Due to the tranquility and beauty of the lake, locals and visitors call Hangzhou "heaven" on Earth.

Hangzhou's 10 Top Attractions

West Lake - This famous lake covers an area approximately 1,404 acres. It used to be a shallow, inlet-like sea. Its cultural terrain was formed in the 13th century. It gained its fame during the 18th. It is considered the spiritual home of most Chinese culture elites, and a haven for many Chinese people at all levels. West Lake was included in the 35th World Heritage Conference's June 2011 World Heritage List.

Temple of Soul's Retreat - Also known simply as the Lingyin Temple. The site is located to northwest of Zhejiang province's West Lake. It lies in a long, narrow valley that runs between the Peak Flown Far and the North Peak. It is known to be one of the country's most beloved Buddhist temples. It was also on the list for top provincial cultural or historical sites.

Qiantang river Tide - This remarkable surging tide is the most powerful in Zhejiang. It runs east to east from Hangzhou Bay. Qiantang River Tide has been described as a river pivot that plays a significant role in the transport of water between the east & the west. It is surrounded with booming cites, such as Ningbo (one of China's major port cities) and Shanghai (the largest commercial and industry hubs in China). The planets' and stars' gravitational pulling causes the Qiantang River Tide, a natural phenomenon.

Qinghefang Ancient Street. This street can be found in Hangzhou at Wu Shan's northern foot. It is located at the Hefang Road, about 100m from the West Lake. It covers an area approximately 13 hectares. Qinhefang's Ancient Street is the only area that has been preserved. It is home to Hangzhou's historic and cultural heritage.

Grand Canal – This manmade waterway is China's longest and largest. Its size surpasses that of the Suez Canals and Panama Canals. It measures approximately 1,200 miles long. In 2014, the Grand Canal was made a part the Unesco World Heritage List. It has 58 historical sites as well as 27 sections. It connects Hangzhou, Zhejiang Province to Beijing. It connects several rivers and contributes significantly to China's primary economic system. Some of the canal's sections are still being used for water diverting.

Six Harmonies – This pagoda can also be called the Liuhe Pagoda. It is located south of West Lake and on Yuelun Hill. It is known as an ancient Chinese architectural masterpiece. Built during the Norther Song Dynasty, the pagoda is a masterpiece of Chinese architecture. Today, the pagoda consists of bring and wooden with exterior eaves added during the Ming-Qing Dynasties.

Tomb Of General Yue Fei- This tomb spans 4 acres. It can be found at the Qixia Hill's southern foot near the West Lake. The Tomb of Yue Fei includes a sculpture of Yue Fei. It is found in the Shrine of Remembrance, its main hall. The sculpture has a tablet with Yue Fei's original handwriting above it. The 373 cranes in the tomb represent the integrity, greatness and faithful mind of Yue Fei.

Xixi National Wetland Park — Located less than five kilometers from West Lake, this park is about a mile away. It is described as a unique urban swamp. It boasts a variety of ecological resources and a rich culture. The natural landscape makes it a favorite among the Three "Xis", which also includes the Seal Engravers' Association (Xiling), West Lake (Xihu), and Seal Engravers' Society. Xixi National Wetland Park combines urban and traditional farming with culture.

Thousand Islets Lake (also known as Qian Dao Lake) is located in Chun'an County east of Hangzhou City and southeast from Mt. Huangshan. Forests make up 81%. Thousand Islets Lake boasts a clear, clean lake and fresh-air. It has 1,078 individual islets that provide different views for every season. It is surrounded with tea, mulberry, and other fruit tree trees. In addition to enjoying the stunning natural scenery and the local culture, there are many other activities you can do in the lake, such as cruising, watching wild animals and swimming.

Wuzhen Water Town — Visitors and locals visiting the Yangtze River south rarely leave Wuzhen. Water Town is home to a history that dates back at least 2000 years. Stone bridges suspended on mild water and delicate wood carvings are some of its highlights. Stone pathways run between the walls are another highlight. It is sure to be an attraction for anyone who visits.

Chapter 9: Hong Kong - China's Special Administrative Region

Hong Kong is found on the east coast of China. It is located on the southeast coast of China and forms part of the Special Administrative Region. The area covers 1,104 sq. km. Hong Kong is the financial, trading and banking capital of the world.

The city is composed of four parts, including the Kowloon Peninsula (outlying islands), the New Territories, the Hong Kong Island, and the New Territories. The famous bays of Hong Kong's southern region have their sea shores. Some of the most popular destinations in Kowloon include Yau Ma Tei. Tsim Sha Tsui. Mong Kok. The Outlying Island and New Territories are ideal for peaceful, natural holidays. Hong Kong Island is the capital of Hong Kong. It's the city's political, economic, entertainment and shopping hub.

Hong Kong's Top ten Attractions

Victoria Bay - Also known by the Victoria Harbour this bay is third in size worldwide, after San Francisco or Rio de Janeiro. This bay also has the largest harbours in China. It houses the majority of the ports of the city. Therefore, it is one of world's busiest port. Victoria Bay is full of all types and sizes of watercraft like ferries, cruise ships, wooden fishing vessels, and cargo ship.

Tsim Sha Tsui: This is Hong Kong's most popular shopping destination. It is famous for its expanding economy. It's located on the Kowloon Island and is famous for its vibrancy, local culture and location.

Hong Kong Disneyland- If you're traveling with children, this is the place to be. Disneyland is famous worldwide as a paradise where you can experience the magic of Mickey Mouse and other Disney characters. Hong Kong Disneyland is home to many beautiful spots as well Disney Theme Hotels. It can transport you to a magical place. Its food is mostly Asian and Chinese and attracts many visitors as well.

Ocean Park – Also known as "The luminous pearl of Orient", this location is a main attraction in Hong Kong. It is also the world's largest financial centre in southeast China. Ocean Park boasts a mild climate and stunning coastal scenery. It is located on Hong Kong Island. It has two sections. The headlands of Nam Lang Shan Mountain are included, as well as the lowlands of Wong Chuk Hang Valley. Ocean Park has a 170-acre area, making it one among the most extensive ocean parks worldwide.

Lan Kwai Fong -- This central hot spot is situated between Wyndham Street, D'Aguilar Street, and Wyndham Street on Hong Kong Island. It is known for its lively nightlife as well as award-winning food. The L-shaped lane connects this famous Hong Kong street with 80 restaurants and bars.

Victoria Peak is located in Hong Kong's west section. The best place to enjoy the night scene in Hong Kong is from this peak, which is 1,817.6 ft above sea level. Hong Kong is described as a glowing pearl at night because of the thousands of lights that twinkle in its streets. Therefore, the Victoria Peak, the highest point of Hong Kong, is the best way to see it.

Madame Tussauds Hong Kong- This museum can be found at the Peak Tower at Victoria Peak. Madame Tussauds Hong Kong, like its counterparts from France and London has exhibits of wax figures featuring world-famous celebrities. It is made up of 100 wax figures. Since 2000, it has attracted many visitors and locals.

Causeway Bay: If you are looking for entertainment and shopping, Causeway Bay is the place for you. It's a popular commercial area on the island with an interconnecting road system. It is both a very popular place for shopping in Hong Kong and a great spot to enjoy nightlife and dining.

Repulse Bay -- Repulse Bay in Hong Kong Island's southern section is considered the most beautiful bay in the region. The area was once part of an 18th-century battle, where the British army defeated pirates. It has since been transformed into a luxurious residential area. Repulse Bay has a long stretch beach with clear blue waters and soft, golden sand. Its water temperatures range between 60.8oF and 80.6oF.

Wong Tai Sin Temple (City) - This Taoist temple, which was built in 1921, is one of most popular in the city. It is well-known by Chinese living all over the world, in America, Europe and South Asia. It has authentic Taoist structures which are very rare in

Hong Kong because of the emergence modern buildings.

Chapter 10: Huangshan – City of Perfect Weather

This city was established in 1898 as a support area for Yellow Mountain. It became famous for its scenic location, which made it a popular tourist destination. Huangshan City is the southernmost Anhui Province city. It is surrounded Zhejiang Province (Xuancheng City) and Chizhou City (Chizhou City). Its most notable feature is its weather. Huanshan City experiences a subtropical monsoon weather, though it can be quite humid. You can also divide the weather into four seasons: summer, winter, fall, spring, and long winter. The city is an important scenic attraction, supporting the Yellow Mountain and other ancient Huizhou village areas.

Huangshan Top 10 Attractions

Yellow Mountain – Yellow Mountain is a famous mountain in China, and it is located in south Anhui. It was originally known as Mt. Yishan, but it was originally named Mt.

Shexian County -- At the foothill of the Yellow Mountain lies the historical and cultural Shexian County. It is located at the southeastern corner of Anhui Province. The county is surrounded with green mountains, crystal water, and lush greenery. It is also home to numerous memorial temples and arches as well as cultural relics. It is a museum of classical architecture that looks similar.

Tangyue Memorial Archway, located in Tangyue's village, is the most preserved complex of arches within the Province of Anhui. It features seven arches.

Qiankou Residence is a section that runs downtown from the Yellow Mountain towards Tunxi and is filled with old buildings. These old buildings are old homes that line the road along a long corridor. The Ming Dynasty was when these buildings were built.

Chengkan Village-This village is known for its colorful and well preserved ancient architectures. Its history goes back more than 500 Jahre. The Chengkan Village is a village that was built in the Three Kingdoms Period. Due to its interlaced streets, lanes and lanes, the village is similar to a maze. It also contains at least 130 old edifices of the Ming-Qing Dynasties.

Tunxi Ancient Street -- This pedestrian-only commercial street is in the Tunxi District's central, where you will find the government of Huangshan City. It has a total area of approximately 1,392 meters, with 979 meters being the commercial street. There are shops on both sides of these streets. They are usually two- or three-story buildings. Most structures are made of bricks or stone base with a tile roof. These are all common characteristics in Anhui structures. Most shops are located at the front of the building, and residences or workshops can be found at the back.

Xidi & Hongcun Ancient Villages – This village is on the UNESCO World Heritage Sites list. They are located in Yixian County. Three ancestral halls can be found in the Xidi Village. These include the Linyun Pavillion. Ruiyu courtyard. Da Fu Grand House. Eastern and Western Gardens. Lvfu Hall. An archway. It also includes 124 historic residences.

Mt. Jiuhua, a mountain that is north of Yangtze River overlooking the Yellow Mountain to south. Its area is 100 kilometers. It is located in Qingyang County, southwest. Mt. Jiuhua boasts 18 scenic spots and 99 summits. The beautiful scenery and the ideal climate make it one of China's most loved summer spots. A number of Buddhists consider it sacred and able to gather there as they do in Mt. Emei in

Sichuan, Mt. Wutai in Shanxi and Mt. Putuoshand Zhejiang

Tangmo Village, Residential House - Situated on Mt. The Tangmo Village is at Huangshan's Foot. This is Huangshan's most famous tourist destination. It was established in the Tang Dynasty. The village adopted the architectural styles of the era. The village is known for its quiet lifestyle as well as its natural beauty, which combines rural life and historical aspects.

Shixin Peak- This peak is said have many wonders. It also contains Huangshan pines that are extremely rare in China. While you are climbing up the mountain you will see the Shixin Peak, the Flying Stone and the Monkey Gazing At the Sea. After you reach Shixin Peak you can go to Bright Peak. This second highest peak is where you can view all five seas.

Chapter 11: Lhasa- Capital of Tibet Autonomous Region

Lhasa is the world's most popular city, due to its altitude of more than 1000 years and its rich spiritual and cultural history. It is situated at 11,975 feet above sea level, which makes it difficult to find and remote. Because of its rich history, however, it left a substantial legacy that allowed for the establishment and growth of the mysterious and romantic Tibetan religion.

Lhasa is the capital and largest city of Tibet. It is an autonomous region located in the middle China. It is located in a valley surrounded by mountains in the southern-central part, just above Kyichu River. It spans over 30,000 kilometers of plains, mountains, and valleys. There are 400,000 people living in the city, of which 180,000 reside in its urban sector.

Lhasa's Top ten Attractions

Barkhor Street- This is where you can see Lhasa's appearance from its inception. Its narrow, paved street is lined with stone boards, which have been polished by Tibetan ancestors. There are many shops that sell their products on either side of the street. Many ambulant sellers line the corners. Many of these sellers and shops sell prayer wheels, the Chuba - Tibetan traditional clothing - unique Tibetan knives and other spiritual and religious articles. You can also buy the Thangka here. The Thangka is a Tibetan traditional scroll painting. This makes it a perfect souvenir. It depicts religious and historical themes as well as scientific and literary topics. Barkhor Street has been home to many items from India, Nepal, and other countries. It's not surprising that there are thousands of tourists who walk the streets every day.

Jokhang Temple – Lhasa has a long history of spirituality. The Jokhang Temple represents the culmination. It is part and parcel of the Potala Palace complex. The site is spread over an area 25100m2. It should be visited by tourists, much like Tibetan pilgrims. It was added to the List in 2000.

Potala Palace – It is only natural that you visit the Potala Palace immediately after the Jokhang Temple. It holds the title of the highest ancient palace. It is found on the Red Hill that dominates the middle city of Lhasa. It reaches 3,767.19 m or about 12,359.55 feet from the ground to tip. Potala Palace is composed of two main structures. The Red Palace and its equally powerful wing, White Palace. The Red Palace, known in Tibetan as Potrang Marpo and is used for Buddhist study and prayers. The White Palace (or Potrang Karpo) is on the other hand the government seat of Tibet Autonomous Region. This palace also serves as the residence of the Dalai Lama. You can say that this Palace houses the culture and daily life of Tibetans.

Sera Monastery – At the foot Tatipu Hill is this majestic monastery. It is well-known for its unique location of rare Buddhist scriptures in gold powder, scent fabric, and exquisite murals in its halls. Drepung as well as Ganden are two of the most famous monasteries worldwide. There are often lively discussions on Buddhist doctrines held here. This makes it different from the two other monasteries. Sera Monastery occupies a total of 114 946 square meters. It is composed of three major structures, Zhacang (the college), and Kamcun (the dormitory for the monks).

Norbulingka, also called "Treasure Park", in Tibetan it is the Summer Palace. The largest man-made park in Tibet, it covers an area of 360,000 m2 (about 430,000 yds). It is surrounded by the Kyichu River and tends to different kinds of flowers. Norbulingka is home to 374 rooms. Potala Palace is only a kilometer away. It's a must-see on any tourist's bucket list.

Chakpori Hill (also known as Yao Wang Shan) is located next to the Potala Palace. Its peak stands at 3,725 metres (12,221 ft) high. You must ascend the winding path, which is typical for mountain settings. Two reasons make the climb worthwhile are the two that you will see once you reach the top. It affords a stunning view of Lhasa, the ancient capital of Tibet. Second, it's the ideal place to take pictures of the Potala Palace especially during the early mornings of summer, when the sun is shining on it.

Drepung Monastery- Drepung Monastery was one of the three famous monasteries in Tibet that Lhasa hosted. It is home to scores Tibetan cultural relics. The majestic statues Sitatapatra, Manjushri Bodhisattva, and Manjushri Bodhisattva are located in the first floor. Rare sutras are kept in the second floor. On the third floor is the location where Jamyang Qoigyi presented the conchshell to Tsong Khapa. Tsong Khapa is represented by Jamyang Qoigyi and Kwanyin Bodhisattva. The sutra halls have flowery murals. This is not only to celebrate the Tibetans' artistic talents but also to represent their spiritual wisdom.

Heavenly Lake Namtso- It is the second largest saltwater lakes in China and the largest in the world. Its altitude or vastness is not what makes it popular. But its clear water is. It is a mirror that reflects the natural light of the surrounding mountains and creates a relaxing and scenic view of unadulterated beauty. It is believed that the pure water of the lake cleanses the soul and spirit.

Lhasa Carpet Factory is a renowned carpet factory that hand weaves its products using traditional vertical-loom looms. The carpets are beautiful and colorful. There are many styles and sizes. Each carpet is handmade in the factory. They are perfect for wall hanging or floor covering. Lhasa Carpet Factory, located in East Lhasa is in the Hebalin District.

Nietang Buddha - No Lhasa experience would be complete without a photo of Nietang Buddha welcoming tourists from Goggar Airport to their arrival in downtown Lhasa. It is the largest, cliff-engraved Buddha statue found in Tibet. It is located 20 kilometers from the city at the Nietang Mountain, Qushui County. A taxi can take you there.

Chapter 12: Shanghai-A City with Multicultural Standards

Shanghai is a well-known international city that draws visitors from all over the globe. Hu, also known as the city, is situated close to the Yangtze River. It serves as East China's most significant financial and economic, cultural trade, technological and science center. Its pounding development makes it one of China's most popular destinations.

Shanghai's multicultural standards attract both locals and tourists, along with its modernization. The city has a harmonious combination of the modern and traditional, the oriental, and the western. Shanghai's skyline features the old Shikumen and numerous skyscrapers. Its unique culture blends Western customs with Chinese traditions, making it one of China's most recognizable cities.

Shanghai's Top 10 Attractions

The Bund – This iconic waterfront is also known under East Zhongshan 1st Road or Zhongshand Dong Yi Lu. Since hundreds of years, Shanghai has considered it its symbol. 26 buildings can be found within the Bund. They come in a variety of architectural styles such as Baroque, Classicism and Gothic. The Bund also includes a long flood-control barrier, commonly called the "lovers' walls". It spans approximately 1,859 meters and is located at the Huangpu River side by side. It is considered to the most romantic area in Shanghai.

Nanjing Road: This 3.4-mile long road is China's premier shopping street. It starts at Bund and ends at Yan'an West Street and Jing'an Temple. It is currently one of Shanghai's most popular tourist attractions, and draws thousands of people from all walks of life, including fashion-lovers. Nanjing Road used to be the British Concession, which was established after the Opium War. It became the International Settlement, and is the most popular shopping street in Shanghai.

Yuyuan Garden -- This classic garden was constructed during the Ming Dynasty's 1577 reign. It can be found at Anren Jie in Shanghai. Yu, in Chinese, means pleasing/gratifying. Pan Yunduan was the one who named the garden after him. He wanted it to be a place of tranquility and happiness for his parents.

Shanghai Xin Tian D - This urban attraction can be found in the city centre, in the southern part Huaihai Zhong Lu. It is home to Shanghai's cultural heritage and historic legacies. Shanghai Xin Tian Di has a pedestrian-only street of fashion that features modern architecture and Shikumen, or Shanghainese residences.

Shanghai Museum – The huge museum is located on People's Square in the city's heart. It displays ancient Chinese art and artifacts regarding philosophy and ancient knowledge. Its square base, and its dome-shaped round shape are a reminder of the ancient idea of a square earth and a circle heaven.

Oriental Pearl TV Tower is located in Lujiazui near the Pudong. It is surrounded on all sides by the Nanpu Bridge as well as the Yangpu Bridge. This creates a representation of two dragons playing with pearls. The picturesque spot is known as the city's photographic jewel. It attracts and excites the imagination of international and local visitors all year.

Shanghai World Financial Center – This skyscraper, also called SWFC, can be found between the Shanghai Tower, Jinmao Tower, as well as the Lujiazui Finance & Trade Zone. It was built in August 2008, and is China's second highest building. The SWFC stands at approximately 1,614 ft in height and has 191 floors. The Council on Tall Buildings and Urban Habitat gave it the first rank in terms both of its usable floor and heights.

Jade Buddha Temple- This temple, located in Shanghai's western area, is a famous Buddhist shrine that houses two Burmese jade Buddhas. Despite being destroyed by the revolution, the statues of the temple were kept and a new temple was created at its current location. This temple was named the Jade Buddha Temple.

Zhujiajiao Ancient Town is an ancient water town that can be found in Shanghai's suburb. It is a popular Chinese landmark with more than 1,700 years of history. It covers an area approximately 47 kilometers2. It has a shape similar to a fan. It is also surrounded by mountains and lakes.

Qibao ancient town - This is the only place in Greater Shanghai that has an ancient town. Its history goes back more than 1000 years. It is located in Minhang District Center, which is 11.18 mi from Shanghai's central area. This city is an example of ancient water townships, outstanding urban planning, and ancient Chinese community.

Chapter 13: Suzhou – Venice of the Orient

Suzhou is an old city. Built in 514 BC it has over 2,500 years of history. It is located in Jiangsu Province's Southern Section at the Yangtze Delta central. Suzhou is divided north to south by Beijing - Hangzhou Grand Canal. A large portion of the city is covered with water that is composed of many streams and ponds. This makes it the "Venice of the Orient."

The unique characteristics of the city from its past are still evident today. The layout of the city can be compared to a double-chessboard. Its streets, rivers, and lakes are situated side-by side. Land and water routes are parallel.

Suzhou's Top Ten Attractions

Garden of The Master of Nets – This is Suzhou's smallest residential garden that comes with the most beautiful gift. Wangshi Yuan also known for the Garden of the Master of the Nets. This garden creates the illusion of a larger area, giving the illusion of greater coverage. It is a stunning example of architecture that creates an atmosphere of harmony and peace for all who visit it.

Tongli Town, a town on Taihu Lake's eastern coast. It covers an area 24 miles with over 33,000 inhabitants. Fushi was originally Fushi's name. Its water township, which dates back to over 1000 years ago, is well-preserved. Tongli is a tourist spot where you can see the traditional culture.

Zhouzhuang Water Town -- This water township has become one of the most recognizable in the country. It is located within Kunshan City. It is known for its impressive water views and cultural background, as well as well-preserved old residential homes.

Lion Grove Garden – Also known by Shizilin. It is located in northeast Suzhou-a City. It is known as one the four most iconic gardens of ancient Suzhou City. The Humble

Administrator's Garden Zhuozhenyuan Blue Wave Pavillion Canglangta and the Lingering Garden Liuyuan are the three other gardens.

Humble Administrator's garden - This famous park is located in China's southern Province of Jiangsu. It is well-known because of its exquisite classical gardens. The Humble Administrator's Garden, which covers 12.85 acres, is Suzhou's largest garden. It boasts a beautiful, ethereal appearance and unique garden designs. It received numerous prestigious recognitions as a result. It is included in the World Cultural Heritage list and was designated under the Protection of the State Cultural Relics of National Importance. It was also named China's Special tourist attraction.

Tiger Hill – This hillock, also known as Surging Sea Hill is located on an area of 3 acres. It is 118 feet high. If you decide to climb the hill you will be able to see several historical sites that have histories going back more than 2,500 centuries. You will find plenty to see and do on the Tiger Hill, even though it is small.

Lingering Garden-This famous garden is located in the Province Jiangsu, just outside the Changmen Gate. It covers approximately 5.8 acres. Liu Yuan, or the Lingering Garden is also known. This was originally a private property with a classical style. It exhibits the Qing style and boasts majestic halls as well as buildings of different sizes, shapes, and colors. It is also included in the UNESCO list of World Cultural Heritage sites.

Shantang Street, a pedestrian road which runs along the river's banks, can be found in Suzhou's northwest section. It is one of the most popular tourist attractions in the city. It is also known "Seven-Li Shantang" due to its distance of 2.2 mi from the Changmen Gate up to the Tiger Hill. It boasts a variety of breathtaking water views and unique shops selling different Oriental items.

Suzhou Museum -- This museum is designed on the theme "Design for China." The entire structure has three floors, with an underground portion. The central and western portions of the structure are made up of a second floor. The buildings are surrounded in elegant courtyards. The main buildings do not exceed 6 meters in height. The museum houses unique pieces of art, exhibits and treasures.

Luzhi Town-This town is famous for its natural beauty. It has old-style homes, old stone bridges, and maidenhair tree. It features traditional female costumes that create a serene, pastoral, yet civilized atmosphere. Many people visit this town regularly to experience the tranquility and peace it brings. Luzhi also has many cultural and historic relics like the White Lotus Flower Temple (Wansheng Rice Company), and the Baosheng Temple.

Chapter 14: Xian – the Eternal City

Xian is also known as Chang'an. It literally means The Eternal City. Because it is in the center-northwest part of China, the city was once an integral component of the Silk Road. The Silk Road records the history and major transitions in China. It is a site of the ancient Chinese civilization at the Yellow River. It has more than 3,000 year of Chinese history. And the city has more that 1,000 years of its own history because it was the seat of several dynasties. Visiting Xian gives you a glimpse into the ancient past.

Xian's Top 10 Attractions

Terracotta Army-- This is the Terracotta Army. It may have been created after the opening of Egypt's Pyramids of Egypt and digging of Pompeii (Italy) in terms of archaeological importance. A collection of statues of both soldiers and horses are ready to battle for the Qin Shi Huang, China's first emperor. It is believed to be part and parcel of the tomb o the emperor.

Archaeologists think that the statues are modeled after the army of Emperor Maximilian. Each one is different from the others. Up to today, diggings continue. The site is 1.5 kilometers away from Lintong, a district in Xian. It is easily accessible.

Xian City Wall – It's considered to be one of the largest and most complex antiquity military defense systems in the world, surpassing many of the finest in Europe. It is also one of the best-preserved Chinese city walls. The walls were eventually rebuilt and expanded after the natural forces of time and change took their toll. It was raised up to 12 meters (40 feet), thickened to 15-18 meters at the bottom, and 12-14 meters at the peak. It is 13.7km long and enclosed by a moat. The main wall is surrounded by a moat at 120-meter intervals. A rampart protrudes from the main walls to reinforce the city's defenses against climbing intruders.

Xian Bell Tower – Popularly known as Zhong Lou, the Bell Tower sits right in the middle the ancient capital. It connects all streets passing by the City Wall, connecting the North, East and South gates. The Xian Bell Tower (or Xian Bell Tower) is a wooden structure built during the Ming Dynasty. It stands 36 meters high (118 ft), has a brick foundation 35.5 meters long (116.4 ft) and 8.6 metres (28.2 ft) high on either side. It serves as an overview because Xian was a vital military town back then.

Mt. Huashan – The famed mountain is located in Huayin City. This is about 120km from Xian. It is known for its majestic mountain range, narrow and steeply carved paths, and sharp crags. Mt. Huashan is composed of 5 peaks. Each peak has its own unique charm and characteristics. The North Peak, also known to be the Jade Lady Peak, and the Cloud Terrace Peak are two other names for the North Peak. The South Peak is at the highest altitude of all 5 peaks. The

East Peak is known to offer a spectacular view of the sunrise. The West peak has been referred to as the most beautiful of the peaks.

Famen Temple Cultural Scenic Area – You can find this temple in the Province Shaanxi. It is located west of Baoji, east of Xian. It is famous for housing the Sakyamuni Buddhist's original Finger Bone. Its history can be traced back to more than 1,700 years. This temple is considered Central Shaanxi's Forerunner of Ziggurat. It comprises four parts: the Namaste Darba, Temple Gate Square and Famen Temple. When the area has been completed, it will be the second Cultural Symbol Shaanxi's after the Terra-Cotta Warriors and Horses. It is also expected that it will be a cultural hub of world-class quality, featuring a Time honored Buddhist Holy Land and an Age old Classic Buddhist Site.

Yangling Mausoleum Han Dynasty – Located near Xian City's north section, this mausoleum holds the tombs of Liu Qui (a prominent emperor) and Empress Wang (a joint tomb). The mausoleum, which covers 4,940 acre of land, was established during Han Dynasty. It is a majestic cultural relic, featuring the tombs the emperor as well the empress. Also, it has a ceremonial area, the north- and south burial pits, graveyard of human sacrifice, and the cemetery to criminals. Along with the tomb o the emperor, there is also a hierarchical social system. In 2006, the mausoleum created the Outside Pits Exhibition Hall. It also opened the country's very first underground museum.

The Tang Dynasty Palace – Also known by Tang Yue Gong. It is located in central Xian City. It boasts a world-class cultural entertainment restaurant and a classical Chinese orchestra. The Tang Dynasty Palace opened its doors in 1988. It has hosted the Tang Dynasty Music and Dance Show along with the Shaanxi Provincial Song & Dance

Troupe. These performances attract a huge number of visitors from both the local and international areas.

Shaanxi Museum of History - This museum, located on the Xiaozhai East Road, is considered to be the first modern national museum. It was established in 1983, and it opened its doors in 1991. It is spread over 16 acres. 207 acres of it are exhibition halls. 2 acres are storage areas for relics. Shaanxi History Museum currently has 370,000 exhibits which display over a million years' worth of history, from prehistoric times up to 1840 AD.

Big Wild Goose Pagoda – Also called the Dayan Pagoda or sometimes the Giant Wild Goose Pagoda. This ancient, well-preserved building is regarded by many as the symbol and emblem of the old-line Xian. It is also considered a sacred spot where Buddhists gather. The Big Wild Goose Pagoda lies in Xian City's Southern suburb. It's about 2.49 mi from the city's central area. It is situated in the Da Ci'en Temple complex and makes it accessible to large numbers. Its simplicity and attractive design are its hallmark. It is on the AAAA Tourist Attractions, National Key Cultural Relic Preserves and National Key Tourist Attractions lists. UNESCO, along with other ancient sites like the Silk Road, added the site as World Heritage in June 2014.

Qin Shi Huang Mausoleum. This unexcavated mausoleum was also known as the Mausoleum Of The First Qin Emperor. The Qin Terracotta Warriors and Horses may be world-famous for their ability attract large crowds of international and local tourists. However, they only make up a portion of the Qin Shi Huang Mausoleum's western section. Visitors from around the world and home are welcomed inside this mausoleum with engraved tiles, bricks with intricate patterns and bricks. You can also visit the satellite tombs that were built in conjunction with Qin Shi Huang. It is also the location where many princes, queens, ministers and prominent persons were buried. The Qin Shi Huang Mausoleum contains pottery figures, extraordinary birds, horses, and other animals. These are considered sacrifices to his majesty. Archaeologists who visit this mausoleum for continuing research find that the relics found in the pits, tombs, and graves are very helpful.